W9-BJU-603

Clearing the Bases

A Veteran Sportswriter on the National Pastime

JIM KAPLAN

Levellers Press

AMHERST, MASSACHUSETTS

Copyright © 2016 Jim Kaplan

All rights reserved, including the right of
reproduction in whole or in part in any form.

Cover image by Vincent Scilla used with permission

Levellers Press, Amherst, Massachusetts
Printed in the United States of America

ISBN 978-1-945473-07-4

TABLE OF CONTENTS

INTRODUCTION

As a guy who chronicles baseball, I should come clean about my own career as a player. In the 10th grade I was a substitute on the ninth-grade team. Not only that, I was so slow that my teammates called me Snowshoes. On to tennis! Fortunately, critics don't have

of reminds me of my golf game.) On Opening Day of the 2016 Yankees' season, the score was 2–2, with the Astros' Jose Altuve on second and one out in the eighth inning. Carlos Correa hit a squibbler down the first-base line that reliever Dellin Betances bent to field. Straightening up to throw to first, Betances found he couldn't see first baseman Mark Teixeira because the runner was blocking his vision. So Betances tried to shot-put the ball over the runner. Unfortunately, the throw also carried over the first baseman; and Correa scored. Immediately, Betances came unglued, walked two batters and gave up a two-run single. The Astros went on to win 5–3.

Playing the game under protest, New York manager Joe Giraldi argued that the batter should have been called out for running illegally on the infield grass. Home-plate umpire Dana DeMuth said the base runner didn't cause the poor throw and offered the Yankees some advice: "Throw it into the runner's back because then what is happening is that he is interfering."

This is not exactly something teams practice.

Baseball insiders also have to be prepared to review and occasionally revise their long-held opinions. For some time the accepted wisdom was that batters should "work the count" by taking pitches to wear out the starter. Now batters should swing at good pitches, since most of today's starters are expected to go only five or six innings.

More than anything, it's the players who keep me fascinated. I can describe most of them—the Americans, at least—in three C-words: childish, competitive, compassionate. (We'll get to Christian and conservative later in the book.) The antics of the men in the movie *Everybody Wants Some!!* are only a slight exaggeration of big-league behavior. You'll be reading about how the Red Sox turned their clubhouse into a golf course during a rain delay. Players routinely dump water or Gatorade onto the heads or stuff shaving-cream pies into the faces of teammates who are being interviewed on television. The Red Sox, among many other teams, have a tradition of making rookies wear women's clothes at some point during the season. And all players will harass teammates once their insecurities are known. Adrian Beltre, a third baseman headed for Cooperstown, doesn't like being touched on the head. Guess where his teammates pound him!

Boys like to play games, and ballplayers are the most competitive gamesmen I've ever met. Ron Taylor, the relief star who became a team doctor (See: Chapter Four), tells what happened while he and his teammates were waiting for luggage in airports. Everyone put five dollars in the pot, and the guy whose bag arrived first won it. Players like head-to-head competition, too. Doug DeCinces, the old Orioles' and Angels' third baseman, was playing a $100 golf match with a friend at Cypress Point in California. They arrived at the 16th hole, perhaps the world's most celebrated par-3 with its challenging shot across water and a safe landing area to the side. The other man had the honor, and he played safe. Whereupon DeCinces pulled out $100 and handed it to him. "Here we are, playing one of the most famous holes in the world; and you want to win so much you laid up," DeCinces said. "Take my money: I don't want it."

What most distinguishes today's ballplayers as people is their commitment to charities, which are frequently more than pro forma. Indeed, I'm convinced their commitment outpaces that of most doctors, lawyers, and business owners, including he-who-shall-not-be-named. Mark Teixeira of the Yankees visited a boy in the hospital. The youngster's parents assumed that was all, but Teixeira continued to call the kid and check up on him. A lot of players are like that, probably no one more than David Ortiz, who received UNICEF's "Children's Champion Award" for his work on behalf of children's health. Big Papi will see kids in field-level seats cheering one of his homers, and he'll hug them on the way to the dugout.

The most interesting player I ever met—and a world-class

Boy, was I wrong! No curmudgeon moaning over modern baseball, Williams was up-to-date and flexible. Virtually a John-Wayne clone, Ted had a voice that carried through every venue he entered, attracting people like flies to wanton boys in Lear-speak. He spoke with such infectiousness, enthusiasm and passion that I found it impossible to disagree with anything he said—even when he claimed that the greatest man he ever met was Richard Nixon.

A final personal note before you start Chapter One. Like many failed baseball players, I segued into softball, where I was marginally better. Early one evening in a workplace league, I was stationed in center field. Suddenly a shot rang out from the batter, and the ball headed over my head. Moving at the crack of the bat for once, old Snowshoes ran it down and made a one-handed catch. It was the last out of the inning, and as I jogged in, players from both teams were on their feet cheering for me. The experience was surreal, magical and mind-boggling—the kind of thing you'll encounter if you give baseball a chance.

Jim Kaplan
Northampton, Massachusetts
May 20, 2016

CHAPTER ONE

Is Baseball Dying?

get down on our knees and thank Babe Ruth for saving baseball [after the Black Sox scandal]," Pete Rose said years ago.

Really? The clubs were going to go bankrupt, the stadiums closed, if the Babe hadn't blustered his way into the national consciousness?

Critics resurfaced in 1969, fully 100 years after the first professional team, the Cincinnati Red Stockings, was established. The previous season Carl Yastrzemski had led the American League with a .301 average and Bob Gibson led all of baseball with a microscopic 1.12 earned run average. The American League batting average was .230; the National League's, .243. Who was going to attend a game when the ball wasn't even put in play? According to a Harris poll, football had eclipsed baseball as America's most popular sport.

"Baseball is doomed," social philosopher Marshall McLuhan told Ira Berkow, a columnist with Newspaper Enterprise Association who later won a Pulitzer with *The New York Times*. "It is a dying sport." Television, he went on, "has killed baseball, and advanced football and soccer. It is the inclusive mesh of the TV image, in particular, that spells…the doom of baseball. For baseball is a game of one-thing-at-a-time, fixed positions and visibly delegated specialist jobs such as belonged to the now passing technological age, with its fragmented tasks and its staff and line in management organization. . . . Baseball is just too individual a sport for our new age."

Young people were growing disenchanted with icons of the establishments like baseball. And besides, they wanted action more than reflection. "Half the people are sitting around, the rest watching two people playing catch," a friend said.

Legendary stars like Joe DiMaggio, Ted Williams, Sandy Koufax and Mickey Mantle had retired, and others like Willie Mays, Roberto Clemente and Hank Aaron were nearing the end of their careers. The lunch pail crowd that had sustained the national pastime was disenchanted with players making big salaries and owners shifting franchises. Other sports like football, basketball, golf and tennis were competing for fans and TV time. And there was a leadership vacuum in baseball, the owners having just deposed lackluster commissioner William (Spike) Eckert.

But a point/counterpoint has always been at work in baseball history. In 1969, new commissioner Bowie Kuhn and Marvin Miller, executive director of the Major League Baseball Players' Association, negotiated a contract that ended a players' boycott of spring training; the mound was lowered from 15 to 10 inches to increase offense; four teams were added; the introduction of divisional play doubled the number of teams making the postseason; and the Miracle Mets won it all. It looked for all the world as if baseball had earned a reprieve.

A temporary one, or so we were told later. Player strikes through the '70s and '80s and the strike/lockout that ended the 1994 season raised supposedly grave questions about the game's future. At that point none other than Sonia Sotamayor, then a federal appeals court judge, came along in 1995 to "save" baseball once more when she said the owners violated the National Labor Relations Act in three different ways. The owners ordered the game to resume under the Collective Bargaining Agreement after its 232-day hiatus. Mark McGwire and Sammy Sosa gave fans another lift with their chase at Roger Maris's single-season 61-homer record. But subsequently the steroid era swallowed a whole generation of stars, McGwire and Sosa among them, with everyone from players, owners and media getting the blame for ignoring the festering sore.

Then a 2005 performance-enhancing drugs (PED) settlement was reached between players and owners, in which violators would get a 50-game suspension for first use, 100 for second and lifetime ban for third. (In 2014, suspensions were increased to 80, 162 and lifetime, respectively.)

The truth is, baseball may have declined at times; but it has

they check out the latest multimillion-dollar contracts with more interest than disgust.

There are concerns about future popularity. The average age of an ESPN baseball viewer increased from 46 to 53 in 2004–14, while football increased from only 43 to 46; basketball held firm at 37. Youth baseball has declined, although a 2012-created Intermediate (11–13) Division in which bases are 70 feet apart and the pitching mound is 50 feet from home plate has expanded. Chalk it up to American ingenuity.

Please note that participation in youth sports has generally declined, thanks to a drop in physical education classes, pay-to-play requirements in some school systems, overbearing parents, distracting obsession with electronic devices and the pressure to specialize, among other issues. Parents routinely spend $10,000 to $15,000 annually to finance promising kids' individual coaching, travel teams and elite competitions. What a turnoff! Nonetheless, some surveys establish baseball as our third most popular boys' sport after basketball and soccer.

Author and baseball historian John S. Bowman writes: "Anyone who thinks that baseball no longer plays that much of a role in Americans' lives should come out to Oakland on a Saturday and come to one of the many public parks and fields where youth baseball games are in progress. My grandson Leo, only 6, plays on a team with mostly 7-year-olds. In full regalia, they complete a schedule of some dozen games. When these little kids step to the plate, they look just like major leaguers as they adjust their stance. Kids in the outfield often catch fly balls or field grounders and make putouts with throws to first base.

"Several fathers of kids on each team are the managers and take turns at pitching (to their own team) or coaching on first or third.

"Meanwhile, scores of us family members sit on bleachers or portable chairs or blankets. Each team member family takes a turn at supplying simple snacks for the end of the game.

"And mind you—while these 'peewee' games are going on, at other parts of this vast public field there are two other games being played by youth or other age groups.

"And this is going on all over Oakland. And California. And the U.S.A.

"None of these people seem to have heard that baseball is dying out."

Indeed, reports of baseball's demise are premature, to put it mildly. Let's put polls on hold for a minute, and let's stop genuflecting to the great god Cyclops in our living room. Of course, baseball is less telegenic than football; how do you televise depth, atmosphere and nuance? Of course, its standing was bound to slip as other sports grew. But baseball has never lost its special place in the American mindset.

The game is always in the news. In 2015, Yogi Berra became just the latest ballplayer to receive the Presidential Medal of Freedom (in his case posthumously), baseball recipients far outnumbering those from other sports. And here's the clinching argument. At this writing, the animated likenesses and actual voices of 68 baseball players have appeared on "The Simpsons." By contrast, just a half-dozen or so basketball and football players have had that honor. And let's not forget Larry David playing George Steinbrenner's voice on "Seinfeld." It all adds up to baseball's total dominance of popular culture.

If mid-season games seem languorous, the one-month postseason is every bit the nail-biter that March Madness is in college basketball. And if baseball is on the decline, why is it so profitable? According to *Sports Illustrated*, inflation-adjusted revenues have grown 24 percent in five years, 56 percent in 10 years and 102 percent in 15 years. Forbes tells us that the average value of a franchise jumped almost 50 percent between 2014 and 2015. Moreover, whatever the difficulties of televising baseball may be—it's so improved, in fact, that every conceivable angle cap-

with Time Warner tops $8 billion over 25 years. Where owners were once talking about losing teams to contraction, there's now speculation over the next expansion. The best yardstick of how wildly successful baseball has become is two decades of labor-management peace. Be assured that there are problems in baseball that I'll be haranguing you about in other chapters, but none of them is baseball's financial health or unique place among American institutions.

Baseball is an unhurried alternative to the slam-bang action of other sports and the 24-hour news cycle. "I like the fact that I get to think between pitches," Andrew Zimbalist, a Smith College economics professor, an expert on baseball finances and a consultant to Major League Baseball, points out. "In a life that's fast-paced, to be able to relax for several hours at the end of the day is a pleasure. A lot of people like baseball because it's an antidote. They need to promote that. One of the reasons I like golf is that it slows me down. The fact you're taking a leisurely four hours is a good thing."

Take a leisurely tour through this book, and I hope you'll agree that baseball is not only a healthy industry; but also one of the best things that ever happened to America. Right up there with the Grand Canyon.

CHAPTER TWO

Baseball and American Culture

(This chapter is adapted from an essay of the same name that ran in the Class Book, Yale '66 at 50.)

In 2007, ESPN's Sal Paolantonio published a book called How Football Explains America. He hit some familiar tropes like the virtues of religious discipline, self-sacrifice and personal responsibility instilled by football pioneer Amos Alonzo Stagg; the huddle as a peaceful assembly producing bonding; the physical struggle to win at all costs; football as Manifest Destiny. In the 1950s, coaches Paul Brown and Tom Landry personified the decade of Ike and "Father Knows Best." Paolantonio acknowledged the violent football connection to "destructive and dehumanizing" activities like the war in Vietnam. He also had some inventive touches: sociologist and black activist Harry Edwards linking football and jazz through "rhythm and beat," and the role of espionage connecting signal-stealing on the gridiron to decoding Japanese encryptions before the pivotal Battle of Midway during World War II.

A most readable book, but which had one serious flaw, *How Football Explains America* came out in 2007. Not even an update for the paperback version through the 2015 Super Bowl could overcome the omission of today's unholy links among football, the brain disease chronic traumatic encephalopathy (CTE) and domestic violence. If football explains America today, heaven help us. Moreover, Paolantonio missed the myriad ways baseball and America connect.

Why is baseball so interwoven into American culture, history and literature? Why is it considered the personification of American values? Why does it tell us so much about where we stand as a nation?

Let's start with the long view. Loosely derived from a game in England also known as baseball, our national pastime actually was a regional undertaking by the onset of the Civil War. The Massachusetts version had some strange rules like retiring base runners by hitting them with thrown balls, a practice known as "soaking" or "plugging." The New York version was similar to

One way immigrants could succeed and assimilate into American society was by playing professional baseball. In the mid-19th century, Irish- and German-born athletes joined rosters, as well as one notable Jew, Lipman Pike, baseball's first leading slugger and one of its first professionals. During the New Immigration of 1880–1920, Americans began to see a wide variety of ethnicities in professional baseball. Native Americans appeared during that time frame as well, most notably Louis Sockalexis, a shooting star for the late 1890s Cleveland Spiders baseball team for whom the Cleveland Indians American League team was reputedly named (although this is in dispute). There were now Latino ballplayers, as well as competitors who had personally or whose families had emigrated from Eastern Europe and Italy, in particular. One sportswriter called Armando Marsans, an early Cuban of the 1910s, "the purest bar of Castilian soap" so that no one would question his "whiteness."

Historian Harold Seymour, author of a magisterial three volumes about baseball written with his (uncredited) wife Dorothy, observed, "The argot of baseball supplied a common means of communication and strengthened the bond which the game helped establish among those sorely in need of it—the mass of urban dwellers and immigrants living in the anonymity and impersonal vortex of large industrial cities…With the loss of traditional ties known in rural society, baseball gave to many the feeling of belonging."

Long before schools fielded nines, there were town teams, factory teams, business teams, farm teams. Success of a local nine reflected its sponsors' self-image, and ultimately a nation's as well. Indeed, baseball became so wrapped up into American identity that we had to say it was invented here. That's why the 1907 Mills Commission reported that a future Civil War general named Abner Doubleday unveiled baseball in 1839 in the picturesque New York hamlet of Cooperstown. Never mind that Doubleday wasn't in Cooperstown at the time. Never mind the overseas antecedents. Baseball had to be American. And wouldn't you know, in 1939 the National Baseball Hall of Fame and Museum opened its doors, in that pastoral village, to celebrate the 100th anniversary of the mythical origin.

During the Roaring Twenties, the biggest names in sport were Babe Ruth, football's Red Grange, golf's Bobby Jones, Bill Tilden and Helen Wills Moody in tennis, and boxing's Jack Dempsey — but it was Ruth who had the lasting and even linguistic power. We still reference a "Ruthian" feat — or stomachache. The Babe was so quintessentially American that Japanese soldiers during World War II yelled across the lines "To hell with Babe Ruth!"

Three major twentieth-century American heroes were Hall of Famers Joe DiMaggio, Hank Greenberg and Jackie Robinson. Center fielder DiMaggio thrilled all Americans, not just his fellow Italian-Americans, when he arrived in 1936 and led the Yankees to four world championships before rolling up a still-surviving record 56-game hitting streak in 1941. In the process he had to withstand some stereotyping that reflected the times only too well. In a May 1, 1939, *Life* cover story, Noel Busch called DiMaggio a "tall, thin Italian youth equipped with slick black hair" and "squirrel teeth." Busch went on, "Although he learned Italian first, Joe, now twenty-four, speaks English without an accent and is otherwise well adapted to most U.S. mores. Instead of olive oil or smelly bear grease he keeps his hair slick with water. He never reeks of garlic and prefers chicken chow mein to spaghetti."

Greenberg, a Jewish first baseman in the thirties and forties, played in Detroit, then the capital of American anti-Semitism.

There Henry Ford complained that "baseball has fallen into the hands of Jews," and Father Coughlin roasted Jews on the radio. Because Greenberg stood up to bigots, embraced his Jewishness, and presented a strong, brave, athletic figure that contradicted stereotypes, author John Rosengren writes that he "single-handedly changed the way Gentiles viewed Jews" and "transformed the na-

rights victory of the postwar period. As any veteran of the rights movement will attest, his accomplishment in the face of considerable opposition was much bigger than baseball. Jackie's supporters believed that if we could integrate the national pastime, the rest of society would eventually follow suit—as it did. More recently, Asians and players from the Caribbean Basin have made a major impact on what might now be called the international pastime.

Baseball has always had magical qualities. A sporting equivalent of *The Wizard of Oz*, baseball focuses on nothing less than going home. It's the only major sport where the defense in the form of the pitcher initiates the action. Unlike comparable sports, baseball is played without a time clock, meaning a game could theoretically last forever. Where there are fields without fences, fair territory extends to eternity. Some enclosed baseball parks are architectural gems meriting landmark status. Writing about Ted Williams' last game, John Updike's famous article in *The New Yorker*, "Hub Fans Bid Kid Adieu," begins, "Fenway Park, in Boston, is a lyric little bandbox of a ballpark."

Jacques Barzun (1907–2012), a French-born American historian at Columbia University, wrote the endlessly quoted line, "Whoever wants to know the heart and mind of America had better learn baseball." Barzun called baseball a magnificent team sport. That's true, but the individual side is actually more interesting. Baseball personifies the American ideal of the heroic (or failed) game-changing individual. Like life itself, baseball is unpredictable to the core. Its skills are so refined that they can be gained or lost in a trice. What's more, individual excellence or failure is sharply visible. In his novel *The Art of Fielding*, Chad Harbach writes, "Baseball, in its quiet way, was an extravagantly harrowing game. Football, basketball, hockey, lacrosse—these were melee sports. You could make yourself useful by hustling and scrapping more than the other guy. You could redeem yourself through sheer desire.

"But baseball was different. Schwartz thought of it as Homeric—not a scrum but a series of isolated contests. Batter versus pitcher, fielder versus ball. You couldn't storm around, snorting and slapping people, the way Schwartz did while playing football. You stood and waited and tried to still your mind. When your moment came, you had to be ready, because if you fucked up, everyone would know whose fault it was. What other sport not only kept a stat as cruel as the error but posted it on the scoreboard for everyone to see?" As immortalized as baseball stars, baseball goats like Fred Snodgrass, Bill Buckner and Steve Bartman (a fan, for crying out loud!) leave an indelible impression.

A. Barlett Giamatti, who squeezed the presidency of Yale and the commissionership of baseball into his 51-year life, wrote, "It breaks your heart. It is designed to break your heart. The game begins in the spring, when everything else begins again, and it blossoms in the summer, filling the afternoons and evenings, and then as soon as the chill rains come, it stops and leaves you to face the fall alone. You count on it, rely on it to buffer the passage of time, to keep the memory of sunshine and high skies alive, and then just when the days are all twilight, when you need it most, it stops."

Onetime NPR monologist Andre Codrescu compared the pitcher to a matador and the batter to a bull. Awash in metaphor, historic and poetic, baseball breeds more literature than any other sport. Ever since Jane Austen mentioned baseball in *Northanger Abbey* (written in 1797–98, some 40 years before the game was "invented"), novelists and playwrights have used it as a central theme. Among them are Bernard Malamud, Philip Roth, Don DeLillo, Mark Harris, Ring Lardner, and August Wilson. Others like F. Scott Fitzgerald and Ernest Hemingway referenced it in their fiction. Editors and nonfiction writers of note have veered into baseball, among them George Will, David Halberstam, Ben Bradley, Jr. and the incomparable Roger Angell. Google "The Web

in the College World Series. "He [Ruth] complimented the Yale ball field, it was like a putting green," Bush said later. He also, however, said, "I was the captain of the team, so I got to receive him there. He was dying. He was hoarse and could hardly talk. He kind of croaked when they set up the mike by the pitcher's mound. It was tragic. He was hollow. His whole great shape was gaunt and hollowed out."

Just as there has to be a little boy in you to play baseball, there also has to be an adult in you to understand it. Giamatti in *Sports Illustrated*: "Baseball has the largest library of law and lore and custom and ritual, and therefore, in a nation that fundamentally believes it is a nation under law, well, baseball is America's most privileged version of the level field."

When Americans need to dig deeply into national pride, they often invoke the national pastime. President Franklin Delano Roosevelt insisted the majors continue play during World War II, so important was it to national pride. As baseball resumed after 9/11, people everywhere cried when Mike Piazza homered in the showcase game at New York's Shea Stadium. The World Series is no longer played exclusively by day, when it could invade the normal routines of schools and businesses but it still touches a vein. "The Fall Classic has become the metaphor for America's love with baseball," in George H. W. Bush's words. "For a few golden days every October each of us becomes a self-anointed expert. The Fall Classic evokes a continuum of memories. We mark chapters in our lives by the World Series we recall."

The Little League and its televised World Series have no likeness in other American games. Fantasy sports began with baseball. Mention the Hall of Fame, and people don't have to ask what sport you're talking about. Election to Cooperstown involves more speculation, debate and post-mortems than any induction to other sporting shrine. That's because the game can be enjoyed on the simplest win-lose plane or on deeper levels involving subjects like framing pitches, arm slots, and scouting. With catchy numbers like 30 homers, 20 wins and a .300 batting average, baseball has long encouraged youngsters to study math. Statistics, which also involve analytics as complex as chess computers, can also produce relatively harmless obsessions. My wife and I were driving home from her reunion at Bryn Mawr in June of 2014, when I spun the radio dial and stopped on a Yankee broadcast. John Sterling was going on about some guy named Dellin Betances. New York's lockdown setup man was getting about half his outs on strikeouts. I began following him, turning immediately to the sports page every day to see how he'd done, rooting for him, and by association, God help me, the Yankees. My fellow Red Sox fans no doubt called me a screwball.

Well, baseball language has infiltrated American idiom. "We got along right off the bat." "You threw me a curveball with that question." "I struck out on that assignment." "I can't get to first base with her." "Arlo Guthrie hit a home run when he recorded 'City of New Orleans.'" "Give me a ballpark figure." "Let's touch base tomorrow." "I'll take a rain check on that." "They don't ask hardball questions on late-night TV." "I started with two strikes on me when I tried to climb Mount Washington in bad weather." Harry Reid on Donald Trump: "He's the definition of a man who was born on third and thinks he hit a triple." (I'm trying to cover all the bases here.) And sometimes American culture infiltrates baseball lingo: Major leaguers use language from the nonpareil baseball movie *Bull Durham*.

You can hear Abbott and Costello's signature routine "Who's on First?" (1936), a comedic classic, at the Hall of Fame. Ernest Thayer's "Casey at the Bat" (1888) became one of our most celebrated poems, recited by Jackie Gleason and James Earl Jones, released in animation and opera. You'll find a DeWolf Hopper recording of it at Yale's Irving S. Gilmore Music Library. (You could look it up.) The poet and

... as far back as 1919, Morris Kaphael Cohen, writing BASEBALL: A MORAL EQUIVALENT FOR WAR in the publication *Dial*, declaimed, "The essence of religious experience, we are told, is the 'redemption from the limitations of our petty individual lives and the mystic unity with a larger life of which we are a part.' And is not this precisely what the baseball devotee or fanatic, if you please, experiences when he watches the team representing his city battling with another? Is there any other experience in modern life in which multitudes of men so completely and intensely lose their individual selves in the larger life which they call their city?"

He went on, "The truly religious devotee has his soul directed to the final outcome; and every one of the extraordinarily rich multiplicity of movements of the baseball game acquires its significance because of its bearing on that outcome. Instead of purifying only fear and pity, baseball exercises and purifies all of our emotions, cultivating hope and courage when we are behind, resignation when we are beaten, fairness for the other teams when we are ahead, charity for the umpire, and above all the zest for combat and conquest."

Scholars say the Christ figure on the mound stands closer to heaven than anyone else on the field. They thrill to two miracles: 90 feet between bases and 60 feet, 6 inches between the pitching rubber and home plate, each established perfectly and unalterably in the 19th century. Reinhold Niebuhr took a fellow theologian, the German-born Paul Tillich, to his first baseball game. Try as he might, Niebuhr couldn't explain the game to Tillich. Finally, the home team turned a spectacular double play and the crowd went wild. Tillich turned to Niebuhr, wondering how a play without scoring could evoke such a frenzied reaction. Again, Niebuhr tried to explain. Again, he failed. In desperation, Niebuhr threw up his arms and exclaimed, "It's a *kairos*, Paulus, it's a *kairos*!" *Kairos* is a layered Greek word generally meaning, "a moment of indeterminate time in which everything happens," according to Wikipedia. To a theologian like Niebuhr, *kairos* connoted a moment so transcendent there must have been divine intervention. Paul Tillich smiled and nodded. He finally was beginning to understand baseball.

The Bible begins, "In the big inning…" But enough levity. Where is baseball today, and what does it say about the country? Please be forewarned that what follows won't be entirely positive.

The longer we travel from 1966, the year Marvin Miller was hired as executive director of the Major League Baseball Players' Association, the easier we forget the game's contribution to labor relations. *The New Yorker*'s Malcolm Gladwell described a telling event in which the model Lauren Hutton picked up *The New York Times* and discovered that the Yankees' Catfish Hunter was about to sign a million-dollar contract. "Why can't I benefit?" wondered Hutton, who was making $60 an hour. She raised hell with her major client, Revlon, and was soon making $25,000 a day. It was not long before the culture changed, and not just for athletes and unionists. Suddenly, Wall Street bankers, corporate lawyers, *Fortune* 500 executives and other talent were being paid like, well, talent.

Don't waste your time whining about major-league salaries. It's hard to find a more labor-intensive industry, one in which labor rather than capital produces revenue. When I last checked, baseball was an estimated $9 billion-a-year business and growing. Do the players who create that revenue stream deserve about half of it instead of the 38 percent they got in 2015? At least. (But, yes, like all rich people, they should pay higher taxes.)

The experience of attending a major-league game has become something of a mixed blessing because it reflects culture only too much. On a midweek night in May 2013, I sat in the press box at Toronto's Rogers Centre watching a game with Ron Taylor, the relief pitcher who starred in the 1964 and 1969 postseasons before becoming team doctor of the Blue Jays. (See: Chapter Four.)

might have objected). The National Security Agency couldn't have done it any better. True, this was a Canadian park and one with a climate-controlled dome and mostly artificial turf; but I wouldn't have experienced anything markedly different in the U.S. Well, perhaps there would have been more fans standing up with signs they hope will be shown on TV—going to the game to be seen, not to see, to experience five seconds of fame.

But paying customers aren't the biggest problem. Despite more comfortable seats, instant replays, and enhanced ballpark cuisine, baseball is in fact mistreating fans, and not just by distracting them from the competition. Most regrettably, at the lyric little bandbox in 2015, it would cost a family of four $336.99 to attend a single game, based on the cost on four tickets, two beers, two sodas, four hot dogs, parking, two programs and two caps, according to the website http://www.teammarketing.com. This is real bread-and-circuses material; these are the empathy and income gaps we see in society. Forgive me, but I wonder how many of the swells paying $175 a ticket for prize box seats would be willing to cough up another eight cents per gallon of gas to fix our highways and bridges.

There's plenty of good news, however, away from the park. Advanced mathematical analysis known as sabermetrics, after the Society for American Baseball Research (SABR), has broadened our understanding of the game. Fans also benefit from better-prepared local broadcasts, ESPN and the Major League Baseball channel, although we must endure, "This call to the bullpen is brought to you by Kia," and "The Yankees defensively brought to you by DraftKings" in genuflection to commercialized corporate culture. Newspaper coverage grows ever deeper, even if it's saturated with arcane statistics like WAR (Wins Above Replacement Player) at the expense of beautiful writing. But there's beauty enough to be observed.

Is that enough? Because baseball has fallen behind football in favorite-sport polls, especially among the young, there have been attempts to speed it up by rule changes like cutting the time between innings. There's also, finally, the right to challenge and overrule an umpire's decision based on instant replay. But baseball shouldn't change itself too much to resemble other sports. As the late Pete Axthelm, author and *Newsweek* columnist, noted, baseball is less of a sport than a pastime: "slow and summery."

Selling the virtues of baseball to a public engorged with fast food and faster entertainment is akin to promoting the incomparable card game bridge over Texas hold'em poker. But it can be done without slam-bam, nonstop action. Just as golfers remember their good shots and bridge players their well-played hands, baseball people swoon over extended hours of insight or what Virginia Woolf called "moments of being." Last season I saw a second baseman go behind the bag to backhand a grounder and with a flip of the glove shovel it over to the shortstop, who caught the ball barehanded, stepped on second for one out and threw to first for a double play. As I write, I'm watching Hall-of-Fame pitcher Dennis Eckersley parse the merits of rookie left-hander Henry Owens' major-league debut for the Red Sox. It's a class in pitching theory.

Having established a PED policy and enjoyed two decades of labor-management peace, baseball displays a stronger, faster and smarter game than ever before. Like figures in the Neil Diamond song, today's players reach the majors rich and poor, black and white, great and small. (I call them "Brother Trout's Traveling Salvation Show" after the inimitable tune.) They're better conditioned than their forebears, care more about their teammates and, consonant with a generation of college graduates promoting non-profits, contribute time and money to worthwhile charities. (I'd love to hear risk-averse major leaguers past and present speak out more on public policy, and more intelligently than Curt Schilling does.) And the marketing is so thorough you could go to Tierra del Fuego or Timbuktu and ...

... now, digging in at the plate, his pants high, exposing hose from the shoes up. The pitcher leans in, looking for the sign. The catcher and umpire close behind him squat as one, leaning forward. The pitcher starts his windup, and the stands hush. But you can hear the music. It's the summer breeze of Seals and Crofts, blowing through the jasmine in our minds.

CHAPTER THREE

The Ignitor (Sic): Paul Molitor's Misspelled, Misconstrued and Misunderstood Hall-Of-Fame Career

(This chapter is adapted from a file of the same name that ran in seamheads.com on December 13, 2012.)

What have you been working on lately?

An essay on the baseball player Paul Molitor.

Paul Molitor. Hmm. Is he a Hall of Famer?

Are you putting me on? In a 21-year (1978–98) career, he was one of the most consistent right-handed batters in baseball. The guy had 3,319 hits, the ninth most in modern baseball and the 10th best all time. He was *The Sporting News*'s pick for Rookie of the Year in 1978. Set a record with five hits in the opening game of the 1982 Series. Had a 39-game hitting streak, the seventh best all-time, in 1987. Ran up these accomplishments in a 15-year career with the Milwaukee Brewers. But he wasn't through. Molitor signed a free-agent contract with Toronto, finished second in the regular-season Most Valuable Player balloting and was MVP of the 1993 World Series when he hit .500—at age 37, no less. His lifetime Series average of .418 is tied with Pepper Martin for second (behind David Ortiz's .455) among players with at least 50 at bats. After three years north of the border, he finished his career playing for his home-state Minnesota Twins, where he had his most hits (a league-leading 225) and RBI (113) in 1996 as one of only 12 American League players to bat .300 over the age of 40. That made him the first *alter kaker* to get 200 hits since Sam Rice in 1930.

Note that Molitor excelled in the field, playing every position but pitcher and catcher in a merry-go-round that at times distracted him from hitting. After moving to center field in 1981, he was shifted to third base in 1982. "Last year they told me I was going to be the center fielder of the future," he grumbled. "I'm going to start working on my slider. If something happens to Rollie Fingers, I might be the relief pitcher of the future." Playing his third position in three years, he hit .302, led the league with 139 runs

ually got less attention than his sometime double-play buddy and fellow baseball immortal, shortstop Robin Yount, who made the majors as a teenager and was American League MVP in 1982 and 1989. "There were plenty of characters on those Brewers teams—Gorman Thomas, Pete Vuckovich, (who became a movie star)—but Molitor had character," Tim Laudner, a former Minnesota catcher, said. "He was just a flat-out good ballplayer: 3,000 hits; runs well; plays anywhere you want." And never, Laudner might have added, made a public spectacle of himself. As former Minnesota Twins manager Frank Quilici put it, "He was private in public."

Where Molitor played most of his career didn't help. Pat Gillick, the Hall-of-Fame general manager, told *Sports Illustrated*'s Richard Hoffer, "It's that small-market thing. Even Hank Aaron was underappreciated in Milwaukee."

Is there any other player he reminds you of?

Baseball-reference.com has "similarity scores" comparing the stats of players and Molitor's Top Ten with comparable numbers are Robin Yount, Johnny Damon, George Brett, Paul Waner, Roberto Clemente, Vada Pinson, Craig Biggio, Derek Jeter, Al Oliver and Tony Gwynn. Here's a comparison of Molitor to the seven Hall of Famers. (I'm including Jeter, even though he hasn't been inducted yet.):

	MOL	BRETT	BIGGIO	CLEM	GWYNN	JETER	WANER	YOUNT
BA	.306	.305	.281	.317	.338	.310	.333	.285
H	3319	3154	3060	3000	3141	3465	3152	3142
HR	234	317	291	240	135	260	113	251
BB	1194	1096	1160	621	790	1082	1091	966
R	1782	1583	1844	1416	1383	1923	1627	1632
RBI	1307	1596	1175	1305	1138	1311	1309	1406
SB	504	201	414	83	319	358	104	271
OBP	.369	.369	.363	.359	.388	.377	.404	.342
SLP	.448	.487	.433	.475	.459	.440	.473	.430
OPS*	.817	.857	.796	.834	.847	.817	.847	.772

* On-base percentage plus slugging percentage

Pretty fair company, eh? Molitor is one of only four players with at least 3,000 hits, a .300 career average and 500 stolen bases; the others are Ty Cobb, Honus Wagner and Eddie Collins. Paul's the only one of the four with 200 homers.

I could get into more obscure categories where he places high, but I don't want you to retreat in embarrassment.

I'm still here.

On a hunch, I looked up the word molitor. It's more than that swimming-pool name in the movie *The Life of Pi*. In Latin, molitor means "miller," and it's more broadly accepted as a builder, an erector, a producer, a contriver, an author (I assume this doesn't refer to a writer but more like someone responsible for bringing something about). The Molitor is a Stradivarius violin built by Antonio Stradivari in 1697 and sold in 2010 for $3.6 million, an auction record at the time for any musical instrument. Makes perfect sense: the guy was a precision instrument who got things done systematically.

Once described as "the most nondescript superstar in baseball," I guess because consistency isn't glamorous enough for some, Molitor didn't get proper respect until he batted that .500, with a record-tying 10 runs and 24 total bases (one off the record) as Most Valuable Player in the 1993 World Series. *Sports Illustrated* called him "The Complete Player" and "a template of the refined ballplayer." Ted Williams said, "I watch him and I say to myself, 'There is probably the best hitter in the game today.' He's the closest thing to Joe DiMaggio in the last 30 years. Matter of fact, every time I watch him, I say, 'There's Joe.'"

After scoring the Series-winning run, Molitor told *SI*, "I definitely respect the game, and that's why I felt a somberness, a stillness, knowing how long I'd waited to feel that. It was everything

ures of David Ortiz, doesn't that inflate a player's career statistics and take some of the luster off Molitor's glow?

You're a tough sell. Let's get something straight. Whether we like it or not, DH is a legitimate position in the American League, and our guy was the best of his time. I'll grant you this: There's no question that Molitor extended his career by DHing in his last eight seasons, and overall he got 43.9% of his career hits as a DH. Frank Thomas, another first-ballot HOFer, got 52% of his hits at DH. After missing some 500 games with a myriad of injuries in his first 13 years, Molitor played about 97% of his teams' games, mostly as DH, for six years before suffering injury-shortened seasons in 1997–98. I can't help but imagine what numbers Ted Williams would have achieved if he'd become a DH after breaking his elbow in the 1950 All-Star game. Of course, the DH didn't come into existence until 1973.

Now here's something really on point. Molitor had barely 1,500 hits by the age of 32. His fans probably weren't thinking of him as a future Hall of Famer, but it's one of the miracles of the ages that he cranked out more than half his hits past that age. "It probably helped that, for the most part, I became a full-time designated hitter," Molitor told Patrick Reusse of the *Minneapolis Star Tribune*. "I was also smarter about stretching, getting my legs strong and loose, to avoid the muscle pulls that put me on the disabled list several times." No longer would he, like so many players, return too soon from injuries he hadn't fully rehabilitated.

O.K., you've built a strong statistical case for Molitor. Now give me a word picture of how he looked, how he played, his life story, what kind of guy he was.

In his salad days Molitor was a handsome man, with thick, dark hair, a winning smile and sleepy eyes: a regular chick magnet until he married the former Linda Kaplan (no relation) in 1981. At the plate or on the bases, he was a coiled and kinetic presence. A six-footer who weighed about 185 pounds, he was regular-sized for a major leaguer, but much stronger than most. The redoubtable Quilici told me, "He's bigger than he looks."

You had to see Molitor in action to appreciate his speed and strength. The description most often used to describe his hitting was "quick bat." That refers, as you might expect, to how fast his bat was traveling when it made contact with the ball. Contrary to what you might think, bat speed has relatively little to do with arm strength or wrist flexibility, although Molitor certainly benefitted from blacksmith-strong forearms and wrists. Physicists who understand baseball say that the hitter's wrists, elbows, arms and shoulders remain relatively stable during the swing. The head ideally shouldn't move at all. As John Paciorek, who had a 3-for-3 major league career before back troubles steered him toward teaching and writing (*The Art of Hitting*), observes, "The 'turnstile' action of a batter's swing allows the vertical axis of the body to remain intact, which facilitates the least amount of head movement. The less head movement, the better the batter can detect the nuances of the speeding ball!"

Paciorek goes on to say: "The front foot secures the ground with such force from the straightening front leg that the front hip is being forced open as the back hip is driven forward with equipollence [equal power] by the aid of a forward-driving back, bent-knee. If performed properly, the vertical axis of spine and upper body remains constant while the hips are rotating along a consistent horizontal plane. The angle formed by a diagonal front leg and an upper body and head as the swing is commencing and concluding is 180 degrees (or slightly less)."

I asked Paciorek specifically about Molitor, and he e-mailed me the following: "I just found a short video of Paul Molitor hitting a home run to center field. I had to keep replaying it and try to stop it at various points to follow the sequence of his mechanics. As far as I could detect, he seemed to do everything correctly. He wasn't a big guy...but from his stillness he must have been able to see the ball well...His

shoulder quickly shrugged upward, allowing the bat to start flattening as his back bent-elbow started pulling forward while his hands stayed back. Then, as the body rotation was intensifying to near 'frontal' position, the arms quickly extended to augment the power already provided by the turning hips and shoulders. A perfect swing, perfectly timed, perfect execution of all body parts, and minimum of head-movement. He made solid contact, and the ball went sailing over the center-field fence.

"I forgot how good he was, and at the time didn't recognize the qualities that made him 'great.'"

Following all this?

Ted Williams called hitting a baseball the toughest act in sports. Now I'm getting a word picture of how to do it right.

So bat speed comes primarily from the torque transferred by the large leg and back muscles to the hips and smaller arm, shoulder and wrist muscles. A good hitter pivots off the back rather than front foot, the better to adjust to the pitch without committing too early. In a hitting video, Molitor explained some of his mechanics. He stood with his feet just slightly more than shoulder width apart. From a slight crouch, he held the bat still while awaiting a pitch, gripping the wood lightly with his fingertips. Then, at the last possible instant, stride-free (he recommended a stride of no more than three inches), he uncorked with a short, quick swing, the barrel of the bat making a straight line to the point of contact. "Molitor's special gift of stretching time until it almost seems to have stopped is akin to the way Michael Jordan appears to hang suspended in midair, or the way players of an opposing team seem to freeze in that instant when Wayne Gretzky pulls the puck around a goal post and puts it into the net," Stuart Broomer wrote in the biography *Paul Molitor: Good Timing*.

Molitor was a noted first-pitch swinger rather than a batter who worked the count but as Jerry Remy, an appreciative opponent, noted, Molitor swung only at good first pitches. Asked if Molitor, in the 20th century, was a model for the taut, simplified 21st century batting style, former Minnesota general manager Terry Ryan exclaimed, "You got that right!"

"One of my most memorable baseball experiences took place in 1992, when I stood right behind the batting cage in Milwaukee during batting practice and watched Molitor take his cuts," Gabriel Schechter, a leading baseball researcher and writer, told me. "Not a single Molitor muscle twitched until the ball was right in front of the plate, when suddenly he'd pivot and smack a line drive somewhere. His feet barely turned; it was all hips and wrists. Fantastic."

Molitor was a fast runner, but his steals came from good instincts and considerable study as well as pure speed. He knew pitchers' tendencies—what body movements signaled throws home rather than pickoffs, what pitchers threw on what count, what catchers were easiest to steal on. He could have written a Ph.D. thesis on base stealing. The fact that in 1990–98 his success rate was 83%, compared to his career average of 79%, suggests that when he was young he stole on speed but when he was older on judgment and knowledge.

Called Paulie by some, Molitor also endured the nicknames Molly and Ignitor [sic], the latter misspelled apparently because it rhymed with Molitor. "Aside from its not even being spelled right, it's a terrible nickname," he said. "I never once entered a room, and my friends said, 'Hey, it's the Ignitor!'"

Those who watched him sparkling at the plate might defend the moniker—properly spelled as Igniter—because of the way he ignited rallies and teammates to perform at their best. "Paulie had a way about him where if you gave him a chance, he could always beat you," the late Hall-of-Fame manager Sparky Anderson said. "He's what I call a winning player, like Joe Morgan. They're just winners." Molitor's teams had a 1,382–1,268 (.545) record with him in the lineup and a 281–349 (.450) mark without him.

cause his family was nothing if not baseball-crazed, he did get a lot of attention. Paul's mother named the cat Camilo, after Twins' pitcher Camilo Pascual. Richard tossed Paul high throws in front of a fence, and the kid imagined himself as Twins' outfielder Bob Allison robbing someone of a homer. He advanced successfully to school, Little League and American Legion teams. The one jarring note—and an omen for his later life—was young Paul's penchant for freak injuries. When he was eight, he fell out of a tree, breaking an arm. Later he fell out of a tree again, injuring a back muscle. On another occasion, he hurt a foot when he tried to ride a bike with no shoes on.

At St. Paul's Cretin High School, a boys' Catholic/military academy at the time, he lettered in soccer, basketball and baseball his sophomore, junior and senior seasons, playing on state-championship teams in each. Baseball coach Bill Peterson instilled discipline by punishing kids for bad practices with repeated head-first slides. Molitor once missed a sign and tomahawked a high 3–0 pitch he was supposed to take, hitting it for a grand slam in the state tournament. "It was a bad pitch, really upstairs," he remembered. "It was right about my chin, and I couldn't pass it up. I hadn't had an extra-base hit in four games. It was a good thing I hit it out or it would have been my neck." This time Peterson was forgiving, saying, "How can you get mad at a guy for hitting a grand-slam home run?" Molitor wrote in his senior yearbook that he wanted to "play pro ball and work with people."

After missing most of his senior season with mononucleosis, Molitor was a low draft pick of the St. Louis Cardinals, and they offered him only $4,000. Molitor took a partial baseball scholarship to the University of Minnesota, whose celebrated coach, the late major leaguer Dick Siebert, aka The Chief, was a stickler for fundamentals and game-situation drills. That was a must for a northern school with a much shorter schedule than Sun Belt opponents, and Siebert managed to win three NCAA titles.

Siebert had cataracts and didn't recognize freshman Molitor when he entered the coach's office with a beard and long hair grown during the summer. "Who the hell are you?" Siebert said. When he realized it was Molitor, he said, "Let me tell you something, Paul, we've got tougher rules than the Oakland A's." They subsequently had a good laugh over the episode.

"We became fundamentally sound players from practicing indoors all those months," Molitor said. Writing the foreword to Joel Rippel's 2012 biography of Siebert, Molitor said that a big reason he made the majors after just one half-season in the minors was playing for Siebert. He elaborated:

"We probably spent a majority of our time in the field house practicing. I think there is some validity to what University of Texas coach Cliff Gustafson was saying about northern programs like Minnesota having an advantage because they worked on fundamentals more. With the limited resources we had, we spent eight to ten weeks in the field house before we even saw an outdoor practice field, so it forced us to work on the minute details of the fundamentals, like pickoff plays. There was not a lot of space in the field house and it was a dust bowl. There were people running on the track around the field, so it didn't leave us much room. It forced us to concentrate on the smaller details of every practice."

Jack McCartan, who played for the Gophers in 1957–58 and later was goalie for the 1960 U.S. Olympic gold-medal hockey team, told Rippel, "For me, baseball was never an interesting sport to practice. Too much standing around. But Dick kept things moving. While the infielders were taking batting practice,

he'd hit fungos to the outfielders. While the outfielders were taking batting practice, he'd hit to the infielders. He made it go faster
than usual. It was more interesting. At the end of every practice,
we had a situation we would work on."

A typical example of Siebert's disciplined yet creative thinking was a play he used when the opponents had men on first and

bunt quickly and get the lead runner, the shortstop covering second and the second baseman covering first, with the pitcher and
catcher also available to field and throw.

In 1955, Minnesota began its season with a southern tour
and beat a Texas team that had already played 25 games. "As a
player, you didn't realize how he [Siebert] manufactured that; but
his teams were better than ninety-five percent of the teams in the
country, no matter what time of the season," said Jerry Kindall,
who starred for Siebert and played nine years in the majors before
himself becoming a college coach himself.

A left-handed first baseman who played 11 seasons in the majors and was an All-Star in 1943, Siebert studied opponents' tac-
tics, read books by other coaches and tried to learn something in
every game before passing on his knowledge to players like Molitor. Borrowing from Ohio State's Marty Karow and Iowa's Otto
Vogel, he freely used steals, bunts and hit-and-run plays to good
effect. Siebert also adopted Hall-of-Fame manager Connie Mack's
practice of filling in a scorecard during games. Seeing how players had fared in previous at bats, he could re-position fielders and
change his offense in later innings. A trailblazer himself, Siebert in
1954 became the first college coach to fit his players with fiber-
glass batting helmets.

Siebert felt players were mature enough when they enrolled at
the "U" that he didn't need rules other than a midnight curfew and

suits on the road. He conducted clinics and created the Midwest Collegiate League, allowing players in the Upper Midwest to play 35–40 games in the summer. The league kept good high-school and college players close by and allowed him to train and recruit them. Here's an anecdote about Siebert's technical style taken from his bio on the SABR website, regarding Paul Giel, a Minnesota All-America pitcher in 1953 and 1954 who later played in the majors:

"Giel told a story to Dwayne Netland of the *Minneapolis Star Tribune* of meeting Siebert back on campus after his 1954 rookie season with the New York Giants and having Siebert pepper him with questions such as how did Leo Durocher defend against the squeeze or how did he work the pickoff play. Giel says, 'I'll never forget it. Here I was a rookie in the big leagues, and there was Siebert, who had been an All-Star first baseman, asking me about baseball strategy.'"

I've spent so much time on Siebert to give you an idea how sophisticated and trained Molitor was at the end of his college career. To be sure, some of this came from his high school and other amateur-league coaches in St. Paul, who were highly respected around the state. And some of it came from Molitor's confident, aggressive style. When Minnesota visited Texas in his freshman year, Molitor reached third, noticed the Longhorn pitcher had a slow motion, got permission from the third-base coach and stole home. "What the hell are you doing here?" Siebert, blind as ever, said to Molitor when he sat down in the dugout. "I stole home," Molitor said. And he stole home a second time in the same game.

After Molitor hit .375 as a freshman second baseman, Siebert called him "the most exciting player I have ever coached." In his junior year, shortstop Molitor hit .325, led the league with 20 stolen bases, propelled the Gophers into the College World Series and played so well his number 11 was retired. For his college career he hit .350, with 99 RBI and 52 stolen bases. "I have made the statement before that I thought he had more ability than any player I have ever coached, and I've coached Dave Winfield, so that's a tall order," Siebert said. Siebert, who rarely spoke about himself, didn't add that it was he who had so much to do with making Molitor such an exceptional player.

Though he was far and away the best player on the team, Molitor and his buddies elected as team MVP the student manager John Anderson, who became Gopher coach in 1982 and hasn't left. "He embodied what we had in mind that season," Molitor explained. "He did everything but play. He was a groundskeeper, equipment man, assistant coach and even confidant for many

big...totally geekish." He was sitting next to Yount in the dugout when third baseman Sal Bando threw Yount an outfielder's glove, saying, "Well, I guess this will be your last year at shortstop, kid." Molitor's reaction: embarrassment, humiliation, fervent wish to be anywhere else.

The Bees were 28–42 over the first half; but with Molitor added to the team, Burlington improved to 43–16 in the last half. He was supposed to play A-ball for only three weeks, then advance directly to Triple-A. Not so fast, said Milwaukee's first draft choice: Molitor wanted to help the Bees win a title! The Brewers acceded. In his 64-game 1977 season at Burlington, Molitor batted a league-best .346, with eight homers and 50 runs batted in, to earn both Most Valuable Player and Prospect of the Year honors. The Bees beat Cedar Rapids and Waterloo in the playoffs to win the league title. Not to be overlooked, Molitor's manager, former National League infielder Denis Menke, made a change in his hitting that produced a more versatile approach.

"He wasn't pulling the ball, so I moved his hands back," says Menke, who would reappear later in Molitor's career. "From then on he became a natural. I've never seen a guy who had better baseball instinct. If Paul was on second, usually with two outs, and the ball was hit deep to the shortstop, whose only play was to first, if the throw was just a little off, Paul never slowed down and headed home. In the field, he would surround the ball when he was going to backhand it. He would swipe at it rather than give with it, and the momentum would take him toward first base. He also had great footwork. Anyone with good feet has a chance to be a good infielder.

"Paul was as close to a finished product as anyone I've ever seen, and I give Siebert a lot of credit for that. He was fast, but he also knew when to steal. Everything was smooth in the field. When the Brewers asked me after the season, I said he was ready for the big leagues right now."

But he was still in A-ball, wasn't he? How would he fare in Triple A?

As Menke had all but predicted, Molitor leaped right over Triple-A. His stellar play in A-ball earned him a trip to the Brewers' Chandler, Arizona, spring-training camp in 1978. He did well enough, but the Brewers understandably wanted to ship him to Triple-A Spokane of the Pacific Coast League for fine-tuning. Molitor was willing and had his bags packed. But as it happened, Robin Yount, who had an injured foot, was holding out and wrongly rumored to be considering a career change to professional golf. As Opening Day approached, manager George Bamberger named Molitor his starting shortstop in Yount's place. In his first weekend of play, Molitor went 7-for-16, with a homer and seven RBI. But what may have most impressed Bamberger was a successful bunt Molitor laid down when he noticed the third baseman playing back. Bamberger said that "nine out of ten guys wouldn't have thought of that. He's a heads-up guy." And one who had to remain in the lineup. When Yount returned to the club four weeks later, Molitor—by now, "Mr. Clutch" to Bamberger—moved to second.

As good as Molitor was, he wasn't shy about asking for advice. "I can remember before one game, when I was coaching with Toronto and he was with Milwaukee," Menke says. "He was slumping and he asked me to take a look at his swing. I said, 'Try to get barrel in front of plate.' He went 4-for-5. I told him, 'Don't ever ask my advice again!'"

"Look at his body," Menke went on. "He never had to worry about his weight. The amazing thing to me is the number of positions he played—from shortstop to second, from second to center—and how well he handled the transitions. When I was moved from short to second, everything was completely opposite. He was a natural."

"It isn't easy being Mr. Squeaky Clean 24 hours a day, and Paul was burdened with the unrealistic expectations of family, friends, and baseball fans," Simon wrote.

During a lengthy period rehabbing an injury in 1980, teammates urged Molitor to try cocaine and he got hooked. It was a handy escape from the image that had been forced on him, and it got out of control. There were times when his family couldn't find him, and in 1981 his future wife Linda told him she'd leave if he didn't stop using. He complied without going through formal rehab, but his ordeal continued. As one of four players named as customers in the 1984 trial of Tony Peters—Molitor wasn't charged, and Peters was sentenced to 22 years—he bore the embarrassment anew. But once he started giving anti-drug talks to kids, calling cocaine "the Devil's drug," all was forgiven. Confession is good for the soul, and baseball pardons its penitent players.

I was beginning to wonder whether he was human.

A sinner like the rest of us. During his rehabilitation he underwent a religious reawakening that changed him. "I believe that God answered my prayers," he said, "and gave me the strength to fight the addiction and finally to stop using cocaine." He references his beliefs frequently.

There's a lot of that in baseball, isn't there?

Yes, baseball is all religion all the time, or so it can seem. Thirty years ago people wondered if born-again and evangelical Christians were tough enough for baseball. Obviously they are, since they've been so successful ever since. People who are uncomfortable with this culture should understand that religion has helped many a player rehabilitate himself from drug and alcohol addiction or avoid bad habits altogether. There's little pressure on non-Christians to convert, although I'll watch the reaction when a player comes out as a nonbeliever.

Back to our boy. As I've said, he emerged from addiction a changed man. Molitor immediately involved himself in too many charitable causes to name here; he was way ahead of the "give-something-back" movement that has encouraged virtually every major leaguer to do good works. Among other things, he worked with Linda to fight AIDS (no small feat for a guy in a homophobic profession) and children's cancer. In fact, he received the 1997 Lou Gehrig Award given a player who on and off the field reflects the character of the baseball immortal who had a disease named after him.

While other players had no compunctions about jumping from small-market teams to big-city clubs that paid them more, Molitor had a wrenching, painful interlude before he left the Brewers for the Blue Jays. He made the announcement fighting back tears. Months later, he called his departure from Milwaukee "very disappointing." Molitor was, and for all I know still is, close to former Brewers owner Bud Selig, who went on to become commissioner of baseball. All of which documents Molitor's bent for considering others' needs: his clubs', his fans', his teammates'.

There was a telling moment midway through Molitor's career. It was August 26, 1987, a few days after his 31st birthday; and his hitting streak had reached 39 games to trail only Ty Cobb (40), George Sisler (41), Bill Dahlen (42), Pete Rose (44), Wee Willie Keeler (44) and Joe DiMaggio (56). The Brewers faced the Indians in Milwaukee's Country Stadium. In the last of the 10th, neither the Indians nor the Brewers had a run; and Molitor didn't have a hit. Cleveland reliever Doug Jones hit Rob Deer with a pitch.

Mike Felder pinch-ran for him, and a groundout moved Felder to second. Dale Sveum was walked intentionally. As Rick Manning headed to the plate, Molitor, who was on deck, said, "Come on, get a hit." Manning thought, "I'll get an infield hit," giving Molitor a chance to bat with runners on first and third. Instead, Manning singled past the infield. As Felder rounded third, Molitor

... himself to ponder what he had achieved.

There was another telling moment in a spring-training game late in his career. Now with the Twins, Molitor was hurting. But when a teammate singled, he tried to go from first to third, his legs and arms churning like pistons, and was thrown out by 20 feet. If an ailing old-timer could hustle like that—and in a game that didn't count, for pete's sake—his younger teammates got the message.

I concede. Molitor is one interesting guy. But you've said you wanted to reserve discussion of Paul Molitor's post-baseball career for later. Well, it's time.

O.K. Stay with me on this, because it's going to be a little while before I actually refer to him. When author David Halberstam asked The *New Yorker*'s Roger Angell what ballplayers are like as people, Angell famously replied, "They are what they do."

But what happens when they don't? I know, I know. Of course there are athletes who have invested well and spend their retirement happily traveling from one charity golf tournament or memorabilia show to another. But there's often a void few old jocks can fill. Referring to Tom Buchanan, a former football star in *The Great Gatsby*, F. Scott Fitzgerald wrote of "men who reach such an acute limited excellence at twenty-one that everything afterward savors of anticlimax." Couldn't have put it better myself.

There's more. Athletes routinely consume megadoses of calories to build up the energy they need to perform. In retirement, too many of them keep eating without exercising and blow up (See: Kirby Puckett). By contrast, when Alan Page hung up his Hall-of-Fame football cleats, he began jogging and lost 25 pounds. Page sat on the Minnesota Supreme Court, an exemplar of an athlete finding an equally satisfying and impressive post-competitive career, until he reached the mandatory retirement age of 70 in 2015. But Page stands out precisely because he's the exception.

Other ex-jocks missing the competitive fix segue into criminal activities (See: Lenny Dykstra). Athletes whose errant behavior was protected or ignored when they were competing become liabilities when they stop (See: Dennis Rodman, Pete Rose). Some former athletes suffer from degenerative brain disease linked to frequent blows to the head (See: too many football players to mention). And jocks who so carefully protected their images when they were hot commodities may slip into bad habits like public inebriation or spouse abuse when they're not.

When the talk turns personal, Paul Molitor refers to the "garbage" in his life. After his 1998 retirement from baseball, when he was, perhaps uncomfortably, viewed as an iconic elder statesman, a Jack Armstrong in repose, his personal life began to unravel. While legally separated from Linda—they would be divorced in 2003—he fathered a child with a woman named Destini whom he subsequently married and had a second child with. Molitor is also paying child support to former girlfriend Joanna Andreou, with whom he has a son. This behavior—I can't bring myself to judge it—is similar to that of countless other athletes. The name that pops first into my mind is Steve Garvey, another admired ballplayer with charitable instincts who has had children with several different women.

Do Minnesotans view Molitor with distaste?

Actually, he's very popular in Minnesota, and not just because people may have tolerant standards for an athlete's private life. His personal struggles not withstanding, Molitor has been a model of the athlete in retirement. On June 11, 1999, his number 4 was retired in a ceremony at Milwaukee's County Stadium. The same year he ranked 99th on *The Sporting News*'s list of 100 Greatest Baseball Players. That being his first year of retirement, he generally relaxed, playing golf, working part-time with the Twins broadcasting team and following Bruce Springsteen on his European tour and...Wait a minute!

...stepped into the television broadcast booth as comfortably as he did the batter's box," Zulgand wrote.

"While many athletes provide great sound bites in the locker room but then struggle in the booth or studio—former NFL player Ronnie Lott comes to mind—Molitor has had no such problem in his first season of working Twins games.

"The future Hall of Famer, who retired after last season, has appeared increasingly comfortable with each telecast. ...

"When Molitor works games...the Twins have their best announcing crew since Ted Robinson and Jim Kaat worked together in the late 1980s and early '90s.

"Molitor has been able to clearly convey his knowledge of hitting, baserunning and fielding, providing the perfect complement to Blyleven, the former Twins pitcher."

But from what you've told me, I'm guessing he was soon into another organized activity.

Right. In 2000, he was Twins' bench coach specializing in baserunning and hitting and eying a future as a big-league manager. At season's end, though, he turned down an offer to manage in Toronto rather than move his wife and teenage daughter Blaire there. What's more, Minnesota manager Tom Kelly had signed a one-year extension and was expected to retire at the end of it. When he did, the old Twins shortstop Ron Gardenhire and

Molitor emerged as possible replacements. However, Molitor withdrew from consideration because Major League Baseball was considering contraction and the Minnesota franchise seemed a candidate for extinction. In the words of Molitor's then-agent Ron Simon, Molitor "feels the situation's so unsettled that he'd rather not be involved in it." His aforementioned unsettled personal life may also have been a factor.

Molitor took 2002 off before signing on as Twins' roving minor-league instructor. And in 2004 longtime Toronto general manager Pat Gillick, then with Seattle, convinced him to be the Mariners batting coach. Some felt he actually might have been more suited to coaching than managing, because coaching involves more hands-on instruction.

Am I right that 2004 was a pretty busy year for him?

Yes. And a satisfying one as well. You can bet very few people enjoyed as gratifying a year as Molitor had in 2004. In early January, newly eligible for Hall-of-Fame election, he nervously waited at his Twin Cities home with family and friends. The call from Jack O'Connell, secretary of the Baseball Writers' Association of America, came at 12:04 p.m., a good omen to Molitor because he wore number 4. Congratulations, O'Connell told him, you've been elected to the Hall of Fame. In fact, he was elected with a whopping 85.2 percent of the votes in his first year on the ballot, comfortably over the 75 percent he needed. "There was a huge sigh of relief on my part, and the room erupted with screaming and applause," Molitor said. "It was pretty emotional."

The selection was wildly popular among Molitor's fellow players. Asked if he was a tough out, pitcher Mark Langston once said, "The toughest. I have to invent pitches against him." Pressed on whether there was a pitch Molitor couldn't hit, Langston said, "Ball four. And you'd better roll it." Asked to name his favorite teammate, pitcher LaTroy Hawkins, who spent 21 years in the majors, said Molitor, because "He ran everything out."

At the time, 3,000 hits was a surefire key to Cooperstown unless your name was Pete Rose. Molitor's brief addiction to cocaine, which may or may not be a performance-enhancing drug (opinions vary), didn't factor into the vote total and shouldn't have. He had a Hall-of-Fame career in his majority of clean years; he never denied the few dirty ones; and he subsequently became a spokesman for combating drug abuse. If there's a message for HOF-quality athletes who used steroids or Human Growth Hormone, it's to fess up and hope for the best.

out and looking down upon it rather than being the one that's taking the call. I know seeing my plaque in Cooperstown will give me the same kind of feeling."

Also in early 2004, he received another significant honor, the University of Minnesota's Outstanding Achievement Award. The highest honor bestowed upon an alum, it goes to people who have been successful in their chosen professions or public service and demonstrated leadership in communities, states, countries or internationally. This is not an award casually given. The All-University Honors Committee must recommend the candidate before the Regents can bestow the honor. Molitor joined a select company of achievers, including former Vice President and Democratic presidential nominee Walter F. Mondale, television journalist Harry Reasoner and columnist Carl T. Rowan. I would be remiss if I didn't include another recipient who's a good friend of mine, David Lebedoff, an esteemed lawyer, author and political activist. To give Molitor maximum exposure, the announcement was made at the halftime of the Minnesota-Iowa basketball game. He formally received the award in April, getting a biographical notation that compared favorably with many other recipients.

Paul Molitor, native Minnesotan and National Baseball Hall of Fame inductee, is a distinguished alumnus of the University of Minnesota. As a student-athlete, he was named First-team All

American (one of only two Golden Gophers in school history to receive First-team All-American honors twice in career). In 1977 he left the University to pursue a professional baseball career. Throughout his illustrious career, he has distinguished himself through outstanding achievement and leadership both on and off the field. Since 1977, he has maintained close ties to the University through philanthropic giving and active support of the University's baseball program. He established the Paul Molitor Endowed Scholarship. As a professional baseball player, he assumed key leadership roles in the Milwaukee Brewers, Toronto Blue Jays, and Minnesota Twins organizations. He made two World Series appearances, [won] a World Series MVP award, and [was] inducted into the National Baseball Hall of Fame in 2004. He has a strong commitment to his community. He played an integral role in helping to bring about the establishment of Camp Heartland, an organization that offers activities and nursing for children with HIV. He is also an active supporter of Midwest Athletes Against Childhood Cancer and the Make-a-Wish Foundation. In addition, he has worked with the Minnesota Twins to create the Molitor Fields for Kids grants program, which has provided the financial support for the renovation of youth baseball and softball fields in the Upper Midwest.

Then, all the while coaching for Seattle and amazing Mariners' players with the things he picked up watching base runners, Molitor painstakingly prepared his Hall of Fame acceptance speech and flew from the Seattle clubhouse to Cooperstown the weekend of his July induction. He'd already had a private tour of the plaque room. "Seeing where your spot's kind of picked out—that is what brought the goose bumps," he said, "when you looked at the other faces on that wall that you were going to join."

"I guess when you talk about Springsteen lyrics, the theme of 'Glory Days' is the older you get the better you were," Molitor told ESPN's Jim Caple. "So I guess that would be appropriate to play. I'll be able to exaggerate as well as anybody."

"He won't have to exaggerate much," Caple wrote on ESPN. com. "I don't know what words will be on Molitor's plaque, but here's a suggestion: 'A terrific clutch hitter, a versatile fielder, a runner as swift as bad news and the smartest, most fundamentally sound player of his era.'"

The exact words on the plaque (Molitor's face is engraved under a Milwaukee cap) are, "A remarkably consistent contact hitter and aggressive base runner with extraordinary instincts. One of three players with more than 3,000 hits, 600 doubles and 500 steals. A career .306 hitter. Ranks eighth all-time with 3,319 hits. Hit safely in 39 consecutive games in 1987 for the fifth longest

als from God to his family, friends, coaches, managers and teammates, acknowledging Linda and their daughter Blaire (said to be reluctant attendees), and nearly losing control only when he mentioned his deceased parents. Beginning his eloquent conclusion, he said, "My dreams never took me to Cooperstown. Like most of these [Hall of Fame members] and probably all of them, I didn't play the game to get here. I played the game because I loved it. That being said, it's the Hall of Fame. It's that magical place, it's that place that transcends time. Baseball is respectful, traditional, simple and pure."

"The baseball memories are great," Molitor said off the podium, "but when you think about your career, the people memories are even better."

O.K., so *what's life like for him now?*

Location, location, location. I lived in Minneapolis in 1967–70 and my two sons were born there, so I'm biased. Minneapolis is nothing less than a love poem to Minnesotans. Novelist Richard Ford praises "its down-to-size, polished and sturdy optimism." This civilized, sweet-smelling city of lakes and parks has everything from notable architecture to light-rail service (really something in a community with scattered population density), to neighborhoods you'd love to live in, to statues of everyone from Hubert

H. Humphrey to Mary Tyler Moore. Hennepin Avenue, once a seedy home to strip clubs and dive bars, has been cleaned up. True, there's a visible presence of street people and drug dealers downtown, but the huge contingent of police and security guards demanded by the business community makes the center city safe. And downtown Target Field, home of the Minnesota Twins, is another love poem, this one to Minneapolis.

Visitors to Target Plaza encounter, among other treats, statues of former players Harmon Killebrew, Rod Carew, Kirby Puckett and Kent Hrbek in addition to former owners Calvin Griffith, Carl Pohlad and Pohlad's wife Eloise. Plus a large Gold Glove commemorating Twins who have won the fielding award, located exactly 520 feet from home plate, the distance of Killebrew's longest homer at old Met Stadium. It's one of many great touches.

Built on a small urban footprint and opened in 2010, Target Field is intimate enough to draw comparisons with Wrigley Field and Fenway Park. The sightlines are excellent. Even if you're seated on the top row of the top tier, you're spoiled because you can look out the back of the stadium and see a spectacular sunset at 9 p.m. in late June. The club's employees satisfy your every whim, with two bars and food choices including state favorites like walleye, wild-rice soup, Kramarczuk's sausages, and "State Fair Foods" like J.D. Hoyt's pork chops. In center field, a large "Minnie" and "Paul" logo shows players in uniforms of the Minneapolis Millers and St. Paul Saints, the old minor-league teams, shaking hands across the Mississippi River. On a state-of-the-art scoreboard, the only disquieting element is a Little Brother camera that settles on couples who are pressured to kiss before the multitude.

Yeah, they have that in San Francisco, too. What happens if the damn thing settles on a brother and sister? Or, heaven forfend, a married man and some woman not his wife?

Exactly. But that's the only thing I don't like about the place. Anyway, a beautiful park deserves an exemplary organization. Though a small-market team, the Twins have won six divisional titles since 2002. Their fans were so grateful that even in 2012, when the pitching collapsed and the club with it, average attendance at Target declined only from 39,000 per game to 34,000. All in all, an organization you'd like to work for.

And our boy does. As a "special assistant" for the Twins organization for several years, he traveled to spring training and minor-league parks on assignment to instruct prospects on base running and infield play, although it's likely he also dispensed batting advice, using his the right

poor judgment errors. But it's his first year of being a full-time third baseman. I tried to be as positive as I could and to help him understand that third base is a position that takes some time, understanding speed of play, speed of runners, when you have to rush and when you can take more time.

"He's working really hard. But overall, for his first year in Beloit as a young kid, he's holding his own. We all know his ceiling is very high—it's just a matter of being patient with him all the way." [Sanó made the big club in 2015, played primarily as a DH and had 18 homers and 52 runs batted in over 80 games.]

As befits a graduate of the Dick Siebert system at the University of Minnesota, Molitor imparted inside-baseball tips. If you checked him out at a minor-league game, you'd note that he never watched the ball, focusing instead on his runners and fielders. He'd tell an infielder that he gave away a breaking pitch by moving to his left well before his pitcher threw home. Or he'd alert a base runner to an opponent's giveaway motion that he's about to throw a pitch home rather than a pickoff. If a left-handed outfielder was going to his right to get a ball, he'd have to pivot before throwing and could be run on. You could steal third against a left-handed pitcher because he'd have his back to you. The players loved Molitor's gems; it was like listening to Bill Monroe explaining bluegrass. And the job wasn't so time-consuming that Paul and Destini couldn't take time to visit places like Carmel, California, during the summer.

Not a bad life.

Anderson, the University of Minnesota baseball coach, speaks glowingly of the help Molitor gave him when Anderson took over the Gopher program as a 26-year-old. Molitor co-chaired the fundraising campaign for the new baseball stadium. When Denard Span played for the Twins, he would work out at the university's indoor facility for the expressed purpose of taking instruction from Molitor. But understand, coaching wasn't Molitor's only public face. Since retiring as a player, he has contributed to his many children's charities and has a golf tournament to raise funds for St. Paul Baseball. But if there's one non-baseball activity Molitor does best, it may be public speaking. You'll forgive me if I paraphrase him a little here.

Two appearances in 2011 were instructive. In a seven-minute address in the public memorial service at Target Field for Harmon Killebrew, perhaps the most popular Twin of all time, Molitor touched all the right bases. Dressed in a suit, white shirt, rep tie and cuff links, he noted the gentle slugger's ironic nicknames, Killer and Harm. "There was no act of kindness too trivial [for Killebrew] to pass by," he said. "He would always ask how your family was." Molitor added, however, that when Destini returned to the table after dancing with the nimble-footed Killebrew at Cooperstown's Otesaga Hotel, she said, "Now I know why they call him the Killer."

To applause, Molitor wondered why it took four years on the ballot before Killebrew was elected to the Hall of Fame. Describing the "mythical yet very real" Killebrew as the first star and designated immortal of the Minnesota franchise, Molitor said, "There was always a battle for that number three jersey on your Little-League team."

The Molitors "talked, joked, cried and prayed" with the Killebrews in Harmon's final days of hospice. Remembering "a gentle, kind, humble man...who put others above himself," Molitor concluded, "Harmon, my friend, rest in peace. I love you, and I'm going to miss you."

At the fifth annual dinner for parents and athletes at Mounds View High School in suburban St. Paul, Molitor seemed even more at home. Casually dressed in slacks, sport coat, shirt and no tie, he got to use his considerable sense of humor and broad knowledge of baseball. After praising the opening prayer ("Good to acknowledge our good Lord"), he said, "Thanks for the intro-

duction. It took m... l... ... ..."

g... y, g..... .... grad Joe Mauer, once an MVP, thrice a batting champion, was playing for the Twins.

Molitor quickly referenced his athletic career. "I was a caddy at Town and Country Golf Course. I'd tell the caddy master I had a Little League game. He finally said, 'Do you want to play baseball or make money'? I said, 'We'll see how that plays out.'" He mentioned his first year in spring training, when a 6'8"coach named Frank Howard hit him fungos hour after hour. "He always asked me if the scout was drunk when he signed me."

"This summer at the induction we'll have a couple of guys I knew." About one of them, pitcher Bert Blyleven, he said, "Bert hit me more than any other pitcher. I asked him, 'Why did you take it upon yourself to drill me?' he said, 'I thought you were peeking back at the catcher [to steal the sign].' 'I never did that.' Bert said, 'I'm still not sorry.'"

Of Roberto Alomar, also just elected, Molitor said, "There was a story when we were playing together in Toronto and we were in New York. The Yankees had a P.A. announcer with a deep voice named Bob Shepard. 'We welcome Bob Hope to tonight's game.' He said. Robby goes, 'Paulie, Paulie, when did Bob Hope play for the Yankees?'"

Then Paulie mentioned a Hall-of-Fame Twin, Kirby Puckett. "There are certain guys you just imagine playing with, and at the top of my list was number 34, Kirby Puckett. I was in spring training with him when he came down with glaucoma [which ended his career]. At the All-Star Game in Toronto, we heard that Al Gore and his wife were coming to the clubhouse. We got the full shtick: Secret Service and dogs. Here comes the vice president and Tipper, going from chair to chair. They reached Kirby, who was sitting with his shirt off. 'Al, Al, this tax plan, what are you and Bill thinking about? You think I want to play this game for free?' As serious as the room was, Kirby changed the dynamic. That was what Kirby was about. I think Tipper left."

"Five years removed from my last game, I got the call," Molitor continued. "It was unbelievable to be surrounded with those guys [at Cooperstown]. There's a golf tournament every year, and I was playing with Yogi Berra. I got to hear a Yogi-ism live and in person. We got to a green, and Yogi had a 60-footer. When he left it 30 feet short, he said, 'If I woulda hit it harder, I'd have missed it shorter.'"

Would Molitor ever get serious? "Everybody gets a fair shake [in baseball]," he said, mentioning a minor-league team he visited that had a 5'2" and a 7'1" player. "Overcoming obstacles will determine what kind of guy you're going to be. I don't want to look at a guy when he's 8-for-10. I want to see a guy when he's 1-for-10. That will tell more abut him."

Getting to the nitty-gritty of his teaching, he said, "Everybody can be a good base runner. There's always a play where you can go 90 feet." Detailing the many duties of infielders—glove work, throwing, cutoffs, bunts, footwork, among others—he said, 'They ask how many times do you have to tell a guy?' We always say, 'One more time,' because some things are worth repeating."

Complimenting the Mounds View athletes in the room for competing, he said, "Better is he who got in the ring than he who was never was in the ring at all." He added, "There's a lot of failure in baseball." Molitor told the gathered athletes to be accountable. "There's nothing worse than excuses. [Say] 'I messed up. I'll do better the next time.'" Molitor held himself accountable for "mistakes in baseball...made some bad decisions in family." In praise of sporting benefits like commitment, teamwork, trust

THE IGNITOR: PAUL MOLITOR

and sacrifice, he concluded, "I want you to support this program. High-school sports were one of the best things in my life."

Pretty stirring.

Molitor left to a standing ovation.

I hear he's still in the public spotlight.

that nearly qualified them for a wild-card spot in the postseason. He was named American League Manager of the Year by *The Sporting News*.

I can see why he gets standing ovations.

CHAPTER FOUR

Bonus Piece
Ron Taylor: Dr. Baseball

(Written with Ron Taylor)

> *"Ron Taylor is one of the most accomplished people in baseball history. He's probably the most unusual and wonderful story I've experienced in the game."*
>
> —Former Toronto Blue Jays' president Peter Bavasi

By and large, retired baseball players rarely go on to successful careers in other fields. Jim Brosnan and Jim Bouton became popular writers. Vinegar Bend Mizell was a congressman and Jim Bunning a senator. Fred Snodgrass was the longtime mayor of Ventura, California. Dave Baldwin got a Ph.D. in physics and has done well in that field. And…and…and…There have undoubtedly been many others, but the struggle to name them proves the point. Before they were rich, ballplayers spent the off-season pumping gas and working other blue-collar jobs. Today's millionaires tend to take it easy and give generously to charities. But from the beginning, ballplayers have been all in with baseball.

One post-career profession baseball can be proud of is medicine. Cy Young Award winner Jim Lonborg went on to dentistry. Bobby Brown, third baseman on five world champion Yankees teams, was a surgeon before he became American League president. But the guy who has ballplayers slack-jawed is Ron Taylor. Before he pitched clutch relief for two World Series winners, he graduated with honors in engineering from the University of Toronto. After baseball, he went to medical school and became a triple-threat doctor with a family practice, a sports-injury clinic and primary responsibility for the medical needs of the Toronto Blue Jays. But let's not get ahead of ourselves. Taylor's tale in engrossing from the start.

The Power of Will

Toronto's Empire Club of Canada (est. 1903) calls itself "one of Canada's oldest and largest speakers' forums with a membership comprised of some of Canada's most influential leaders from the professions, business, labour, education and government." Among the eminences who have addressed it are Winston Churchill,

of the Spencer Stuart corporate head-hunting firm, and a Superior Court justice.

Then he turned to the business of the day's speaker. Referencing "one man's remarkable odyssey through life and the lessons he learned," he describes a man with three lives ("a rather nice cat in disguise") who earned a degree with honors in engineering, threw $4^2/_3$ innings of no-hit relief against the Yankees in the World Series, graduated from medical school at age 40 and went on to become team doctor for the Toronto Blue Jays.

And so the 66-year-old Ron Taylor, in a suit, white shirt and tie, took the podium. With a nose round on the sides, wide and flat on top, he resembled a handsomer version of the actor Karl Malden, who won an Academy Award for Best Supporting Actor in *A Streetcar Named Desire* and played a detective in TV's "Streets of San Francisco." Avoiding eye contact, barely moving his lips, Taylor began, "We've got the first five minutes covered [meaning his introduction]. Where do we go from here?"

The audience appreciated his wry humor and laughed. Then he launched into an account of his life. "I was playing amateur baseball in Leaside [a Toronto neighborhood] and pitched batting practice for the Toronto Maple Leafs [a Triple-A minor league team]." His schoolboy success impressed a sheet-metal worker named Chester Dies who was a Cleveland Indians scout. In late summer of 1955 Dies called Cleveland executives who showed no interest, so he paid for two train tickets and took the 17-year-old Taylor to Cleveland.

"We got to Cleveland, checked into a hotel, got up the next morning, and we had a root-beer float for breakfast," Taylor continued to more laughter.

Dies told the director of player development, Laddie Placek, "I've got this kid from Toronto who throws very hard" and got chewed out for bringing him in without permission. "I said, 'This isn't going the way I thought it would,'" Taylor said to chuckles.

The farm director said, Taylor remembered, "Well, since you're here, I'll let the kid pitch to the bullpen catcher and you can take him home tomorrow."

"I wasn't very smart, but I could throw hard," Taylor said. So hard that the bullpen catcher alerted pitching coach Mel Harder. The next day Taylor threw for Manager Al Lopez, a future Hall of Famer. And on Labor Day, Taylor pitched batting practice to the likes of Vic Wertz, Al Rosen and Larry Doby, veterans of the 1954 pennant winners.

Suddenly, the Indians wanted to sign the kid to a contract! At the time, baseball had a system in which players signing rich pacts were considered "bonus babies" who had to remain on the big-league roster for two years. It was a terrible system (long-since abolished) because youngsters logically needed to spend some time in the minors before being promoted. Even future Hall of Famers like Sandy Koufax and Harmon Killebrew had their careers sidetracked because of the rule. Taylor understood this and said, "I want to get the maximum you can get" short of the bonus-baby range. That was $4,000, and the Indians signed him for that amount. "They flew us back on a DC-3," Taylor said. He would spend $2,900 of the bonus on his college education.

Taylor had already been trained as a fighter-squadron airman in the Royal Canadian Air Force, but he gave up his dream of becoming a pilot to take the Indians' offer. In 1956, he reported to their minor-league training camp. "There were 250 players, and my number was 247," he said to more laughter from the Empire Club audience. "I knew T is low on the alphabet, but not that low."

The audience was in his back pocket now. "There was a guy with his locker in front of me. Number 9. He was very friendly and kind to me. That was Roger Maris."

While earning $250 a month, Taylor won 17 games with a 3.13 ERA and pitched 227 innings at age 18 for the Daytona Beach Islanders of the Florida State League. He was playing at the l...... .... .f .l... ... .

... . g.... .. ... g.. .... years of engineering."

"We can put you in Case Institute here in Cleveland on the semester system," Placek said.

"I want to get it over with [and study full-time in Toronto]. ... But I will play baseball for you in the summer. I just won't go to spring training."

Placek gagged. "I had him on the hook," Taylor said, 'cause I won 17 games."

"He said, 'O.K., we'll go for that.'"

Taylor progressed through the minor leagues — Class-C Fargo-Moorhead (N.D.) Twins, 1957; Class-C Minot (N.D.) Mallards, 1958; Single-A Reading (PA) Indians, 1959–60 — while studying electrical engineering at the University of Toronto. He graduated in 1961 with First-Class Honours — in engineering and, apparently, chutzpah. "I said to Cleveland, 'I've got a lot of job offers,' which I really didn't have [laughter], 'but I'd really like to play baseball. I want an invitation to the big-league camp.'" After finishing the 1961 season with the Triple-A Salt Lake City Bees, he got it.

"I was number 66 in Tucson. I'm moving up the ladder. I pitched 26 scoreless innings in spring training and made the club."

In the second game of the season, Taylor and Boston's Bill Monbouquette threw 11 scoreless innings before Carroll Hardy beat Taylor with a grand slam in the 12th. Thirteen days later

Taylor beat another good pitcher, Dean Chance, 3–2, throwing $6^1/_3$ innings. Eventually the hitters caught up to the off-speed pitches he hadn't mastered yet and Taylor was demoted to the Jacksonville Suns of the International League. He finished the year there, loved the hot weather and played for pennant winners as one of best (12–4, 2.62) pitchers in the league. While he was playing for San Juan, Puerto Rico in the winter leagues, Cardinal manager Johnny Keane scouted him and got the Indians to trade him to St. Louis.

"I was going to be the [Cardinals'] fourth starter. They put my locker next to Stan Musial's. He was on my right, and I'm looking for all this fatherly advice. He said, 'Kid, if you want to get your shoes shined, put them next to my locker. I'm a big tipper.' I said, 'Thanks, Stan, that's great.'" Musial did much, though, to make Taylor comfortable on a veteran club.

Taylor started nine games, winning twice. When the Cardinals saw that he could pitch many innings and had developed a sinker-slider repertoire ideal for producing ground balls off the bat, they used him in relief, where he hid his disappointment at not start-ing and won seven more games and unofficially saved 11. (Before 1969, any pitcher entering a game with a lead and finishing with a lead still intact qualified for a save. The statistic wasn't official and was rarely cited.) Then he returned to Toronto to work as an engineer.

"The following year we won it [the 1964 pennant]. People ask what it's like when you're in a tight situation and the manager comes out to talk to you. I remember one. Johnny Keane is the manager, and he brings me in with the bases loaded, and the hitter is Willie Mays. [Actually, there were two runners on, but that was pressure enough.] I walk in. And he says, 'Now listen.'

"'I think, "I'm listening, Johnny."'

"'The bases are loaded.'

"'I already know that, John.'

"'The hitter is Willie Mays.'

"'I had that figured out, too, Johnny.'

"'Don't give him anything to hit, but don't walk him.'"

Taylor got Mays out.

The Cardinals won the pennant on the last day of the season and played the Yankees in the World Series. "We're down two games to one, and the Yankees get three runs in the first inning. If we lose this game, we're toast because we have another game in Yankee Stadium the next day. Our third baseman, Ken Boyer, hit a grand slam in the top of the sixth. I was warming up and all these

walked up. I just saw Tim's glove. There was no sound, just us playing catch, and I pitch four innings with no hits and we went on to win the World Series. That was very good." He's greeted with laughter and applause.

Midway through a bad season in 1965, Taylor was traded to the Houston Astros. "They [the Cardinals] wanted a left-handed pitcher. There was a press conference and they asked 'What do you think of the trade, Ronnie?' I said, 'It was a bad trade for both clubs.' That one kind of shortened my stay in Houston." Laughter.

The ground balls that Taylor induced bounced off the cement-like Astroturf like lacrosse balls, and over infielders' heads. He had back trouble to boot. After the 1966 season, he was demoted to Oklahoma City, then signed by the dog-eared New York Mets, perennial cellar-dwellers. Taylor consoled himself, figuring New York would be better than Houston with its comparatively mild summers and beautiful grass infield.

"Casey Stengel was a vice president, and he would hold a break-camp meeting for the players. He said, 'You are the New York Metropolitans. You represent the biggest city in North America. We got a great ball club here. We got Tom Seaver. Tom Seaver is 22; in 10 years he will be an All-Star pitcher perennially. Over here we got Nolan Ryan. Nolan Ryan is 20, and he throws the ball 100 miles an hour; in 10 years he will be a Hall of Famer.

Over here we got Jerry Koosman. Jerry Koosman is 24. In 10 years he will be the best left-hander in the National League. And over here we got Ron Taylor. We just got Ron Taylor in a trade with Houston. Ron Taylor is 27. In 10 years, if he takes care of himself, he'll be 37.'" Laughter and applause. [Taylor later admitted the story was apocryphal, but Stengel definitely told it about a player named Greg Goosen.]

"We head north. Get into New York, and there was a rainout. Half the team held a victory party." Laughter. "We finished last. [He didn't mention that he led Mets relievers with eight saves, two of them by the pre-1969 definition, a 2.34 ERA and 50 appearances.] The following year [1968] Gil Hodges came in. What he did was establish everyone's responsibilities. Everything started to gel. Young pitchers like Seaver and Koosman and Ryan came along, and this old [30] guy Taylor came along, too [with 14 saves and a 2.70 ERA]. ... And the following year we won the pennant."

Taylor described one game: "Gil Hodges called me in from the bullpen. It was a slight drizzle, and Gil came out and he was singing 'Raindrops Keep Falling on My Head.' And he said, 'Listen, we got first base open. [Henry] Aaron's up, I want you to put Aaron on and pitch to [Orlando] Cepeda.'

"I said, 'No, I want to pitch to Henry.'

"'You what?'

"'I want to pitch to Henry. I'll get him out.'

"He said, 'You better.'"

With a 2–0 count, Hodges changed his mind and signaled to Taylor to walk Aaron. Then Taylor retired Cepeda. On the bench after the game, Hodges looked at Taylor and shook his head in wonderment.

"Another time I was pitching, and I got a line drive off my head. I'm looking for the ball all around. I hear one roar go up, and then another went up. And then Hodges came out, and he's laughing ... He said, 'How do you feel?' I used to always say to him. 'I never felt better.' This time I said, 'If I felt any better, it would be criminal.'

"So he said, 'You just got a double play off your head. That's an assist for you.' He said, 'Get the next guy out.' He left me in.

Now we'd Medevac the guy to the hospital."

Taylor fast-forwarded through the postseason, in which he had a win and completed a game to preserve Tom Seaver's win in the 1969 National League playoffs. He kept the Mets in the Series opener they lost and saved Game Two by retiring Brooks Robinson, the only batter he faced, with a one-run lead, two men on

Taylor played two more seasons with the Mets and retired in 1972 after his arm went dead in a brief stint with San Diego. In three USO trips he'd taken to visit injured soldiers in the Far East, Taylor was impressed by the power of doctors to do good. As a favor for old friend Bill Forder, a urological surgeon who had been encouraging Taylor to pursue his interest in medicine, the associate dean of student affairs at the University of Toronto Medical School granted Taylor an interview. "I said, 'I'd like to sign up for medical school.'

"'He said, 'You would.'"

"'I would.'

"He said, 'We have several applicants for about 200 spots. ... How old are you?'

"'Thirty-four.'

"'What have you been doing?'

"'I've been playing major-league baseball."

"'What's that?' I knew I was in trouble.

"He said, 'While you're here, let me look at your transcript.' I did very well in engineering.

"He looked at it. He looked at me. 'Are these [grades] yours?'

"'Yeah.'

"He shook his head. He said, 'I'll tell you what. If you were 24, we'd let you in. But you're 34. What I'd suggest to you is to go back and take honor courses in biology, microbiology and chemistry. If you get the same grades, we'll consider your application.'

"'What are the odds?'

"He said, 'Well, it depends on the person on the admissions committee. I'd say about 50–50.'

"'Those are pretty good odds. I'll take it.'"

Living at his father's house (his mother had died), Taylor moved into his sister's old room, virtually bare but for a mattress and drafting table he piled his books on. Standing up to study because of his old back injury, he worked on concentrating. The courses were all about memorization. He hadn't been in school for more than 10 years. This was a challenge in its own way as tough as facing the Cardinals and Orioles in the World Series.

"I'd go to school from 8 to 5, sleep till 10 and [study] from 10 [p.m.] to 7 [a.m.]. I did that all year, got good grades and was admitted to medical school." A letter of recommendation from Mets board chairman M. Donald Grant, a native Montrealer, didn't hurt.

"I show up at medical school." He walked in, and the class thought he was a school employee. The joke going around was:

"How do you get into medical school?"

"Get straight A's or be a washed-up baseball player."

"I got through medical school O.K., and I became an intern. We'd go around in clinical groups, and the professor thought I was a volunteer patient." Laughter. "I got through it and got my license to practice medicine."

Not only that, but Taylor started a sports-injuries clinic and became team doctor for the Toronto Blue Jays. There had been ballplayers who became doctors, but never before a team doctor. "I've been fortunate in every career job I've had," Taylor said. "I always ask my patient, 'How's your job coming along?' A lot of times people who aren't having fun at their jobs have health problems."

It was time to wind down. Taylor described his father's Irish ancestry and his mother's Welsh antecedents. "My mother missed the boat to Australia, and they came to Canada." Laughter. "I'm glad I'm here." Laughter and applause. "God bless Ireland, God bless Welshland and God bless North Americaland. Thank you."

Taylor got a standing ovation. John Koopman, past president of the Empire Club, said, "That was a wonderful story, told with humility and a tremendous amount of entertainment. That was one of the best speeches we've heard at the Empire Club for many years, and I've been here 40 years. ...

"Dr. Taylor has ...

... said it was the best speech they'd heard at the Empire Club. Taylor had gone through his extraordinary life in about 18 minutes. But there was more. Much more.

Luck and Pluck

Ron Taylor ascribes his success to luck as well as pluck. Well, he was certainly fortunate to come from tough immigrant stock. His paternal grandfather Walter and his wife Elizabeth moved from Ireland to Flesherton, Ontario, and became farmers. They eventually relocated to Toronto, where Walter ran a confectionary, W. Taylor Cash & Confectioners, and was a streetcar driver for the Toronto Transit Commission while he and Elizabeth raised five children. And Ron's maternal grandfather William Evans, a Welshman, fought in the Battle of Mafeking in the turn-of-the-century Boer War as a cavalry soldier under Colonel Robert Baden-Powell. Later, he ran the Red Lion Pub in Welshpool, Wales. After his death, his widow Emily took the family, including Ron's mother Maude, to Canada. It's not absolutely clear whether they really missed the boat to Australia—that's a nice story—or opted for Canada.

Young Wesley Taylor, Ron's father, came of age in hard times. When he was 13, his father Walter died in the 1919 worldwide flu epidemic, forcing Wesley to leave school and support his four siblings and mother. He got a job with Dunlop Tire and Rubber that he maintained through the Depression and beyond, retiring after half a century as an auto-parts salesman. Having missed out on a standard education, Wesley took night courses and stressed the value of study to Ron and his older sister Carole. A photo in Ron's house shows a distinguished, gray-haired man active in the Leaside athletic association.

Ron inherited his mother's considerable intelligence. He swears Maude could read a chapter of Hemingway and recite the whole thing from memory. In an age when women weren't expected to hold jobs, Maude was frustrated and angry. No doubt there were tensions within the marriage. Lovingly preserved in Taylor's scrapbook are the remains of the marriage license Wesley tore up during a marital spat. But he and Maude stayed together.

"I realized how brilliant she was, and how it was wasted," Ron says. "It made me realize that if you take advantage of opportunities, you can achieve." He didn't realize it at the time, but through hard work and focus he would achieve significantly in three disparate disciplines. Those features—hard work and focus—are the primary factors in his life's work.

There was more good fortune, although it didn't seem so at the time. Soon after Ron was born on December 13, 1937, he suffered an anemic condition that produced a clotting disorder resulting in constant nosebleeds and transfusions. "The doctor came over and told us, 'You give him a big hug because you might not see him again,'" Ron's sister Carole, who had a career as a Prudential secretary, remembers. The clotting stopped when Ron was seven. "And later he had scarlet fever," Carole says. "My whole class came up and sang him Christmas carols."

Lucky? Yes, because, Ron didn't strap on skates until he was seven. Since professional hockey players virtually skate out of the womb, it was already too late for Ron to succeed in Canada's favorite sport. And that was fine because he was much more suited for baseball. Supposedly, Ron was a natural lefty; but his mother feared heart problems if he overused his left side and made him switch to right-handed. Ron has no memory of the switch, but it's another nice story. Meanwhile, Ron's father, a former sandlot infielder who was more successful as a speedskater, spent hours catching him, stressing control. "We had a kind of plate and the driveway had a slope, so it was like pitching off a mound," Taylor says.

Once Ron started competing at Talbot Park, his mother worked the concession booth. "She was some fan," Carole says.

Anselm Catholic School. He didn't go there. Enter Phil Stein. A workhorse goalie for 13 minor-league seasons who played one game for the 1939–40 Toronto Maple Leafs (a 2–2 tie), Stein was now retired from hockey and working as recreation director at Leaside. "Phil made an exception and let me play for the Leaside teams," Taylor says. "He changed my life. By getting on a team, I had a real sense of achievement. He taught us the fundamentals of baseball and sportsmanship. He was at my side all the way up. I always made sure that if I was getting an award, I'd invite him."

Now, it's tempting to say that Canadians don't dominate major-league baseball because the weather up North is lousy. And you might wonder how players like Ron succeeded when the sport wasn't offered in his schools at the time. (Taylor played basketball and football.)

Actually, Canadian baseball has a distinguished history. A five-base game resembling baseball was played on June 4, 1838, in Ontario's Oxford Country between teams from Beachville and Zorra. According to baseball-reference.com, Bob Addy was the first Canadian to play in the majors, with Rockford, Illinois, in 1871. James Edward (Tip) O'Neill, of Woodstock, Ontario, won baseball's first triple crown for the St. Louis Browns in 1887 and hit .326 over 10 seasons. Bill Galloway, of the Canadian League's Woodstock, Ontario team, in 1899 was the last black to play in

an integrated Canadian league before Jackie Robinson, who him-
self played a minor-league season in Montreal. Another African-
American, Elston Howard, was the International League's Most
Valuable Player with the 1954 Toronto Maple Leafs.

Canadian ballplayers benefit from the hockey mentality: grit,
heart, toughness, unselfishness. Canadians eat dirt, block balls
with their faces, run through fences, at least metaphorically. Describing someone they like, say, Derek Jeter crashing into the seats
in pursuit of a pop-up, old-time baseball men may say, "He plays
Canadian." So it should be no surprise that players like MVPs
Larry Walker, Joey Votto and Justin Morneau, Rookie of the Year
Jason Bay, Cy Yong Award winner Eric Gagne and Hall-of-Fame
pitcher Ferguson Jenkins hail from north of the border. Canada
won the World Youth Baseball Championship in 1991, beating
Chinese Taipei, 5–2, in the finals. One of 135 teams trying to
qualify for the 2004 Olympics, Canada made the Greek games
and finished fourth, nearly qualifying for the gold-medal game.
Lately there's been a notable influx of players from warm(er)-
weather British Columbia, where a February-through-October
season benefits athletes who already play Canadian.

In addition, Canadians have contributed to the majors as
coaches, umpires, managers, owners and other executives. Doug
Melvin (Brewers), Gord Ash (Blue Jays), Murray Cook (Expos and
Reds) and George Selkirk (Washington Senators) were GMs. Paul
Beeston was president of Major League Baseball from 1997 to
2002. Between 1871 and 1933 five Canadians — George Gibson,
Arthur Irwin, Fred Lake, Bill Watkins and Jimmy Wood — man-
aged in the majors. An orphan at 14 who walked from Quebec
City to Boston and became a commodities millionaire, Red Sox
owner (1914–16) J. J. Lannin of Lac-Beauport, Quebec, signed
Babe Ruth and shepherded two World Series winners.

Some interesting generalizations apply to Canadian ballplayers. More of them bat left-handed than other hitters, because
they've played hockey left-handed. Canadians tend to play corner positions in the infield and outfield rather than finesse ones
because they're so physical. They're not known for speed, having
played hockey flat-footed on skates. And they get nicknames that

range from the corny ("Big" for a guy 6' 6") to inventive ("Hair Pin" for a player wound so tight he could snap like a hair pin off a woman's head).

When Taylor was developing as a player in the late Forties and early Fifties, Canadians did a terrific job training young players through dedicated coaches, first-rate youth and municipal leagues,

Taylor found serenity in baseball that wasn't always there at home, given his parents' turbulent marriage. At the ballfield, all was in order. His mother ran the concession stand, while his father was one of Ron's coaches. Without external influences distracting him, he could focus on games and let other things drift away. Let's fast-forward to 1950, when 12-year-old Ron and his Leaside Rotary Pee Wee Cubs competed for three championships. First, they won the Leaside Baseball Association title. Ron was the number two pitcher behind Billy Kennedy, who later played pro hockey, and Ron played outfield when he wasn't pitching. Both Taylor and Kennedy pitched to catcher Charlie Burns, who later played hockey with the Boston Bruins. Advancing to the Toronto Minor Baseball Association playoffs, Taylor retired the first 20 batters he faced, with 12 strikeouts and no walks, while beating an inexperienced Runnymede team, 22–2; and Kennedy added another lopsided win to advance a round. Against Pape, Taylor threw a three-hitter but lost, 5–2. "It was lost mainly by an attack of nerves by the whole team," one of the coaches, Frank Kronk, wrote in a booklet he created about the postseason. Leaside got even, 4–3, when Kennedy won in an extra-inning nail-biter. At the end, Kronk wrote, "The ball got loose for a few seconds and we all died a thousand deaths thinking Richardson was going to score; but Green recovered in time." Leaside won the rubber game, 10–4, and Kronk exulted, "In this game the team seemed to find themselves. The jitters and nervousness had disappeared, even the manager and coach were back to normal."

Before the final, against Sportsman, an opposing pitcher named Spider Brown told Mr. and Mrs. Taylor, "Leaside has a nice team; however, we will take them two straight to win the T.M.B.A." Kronk wrote, "When this remark was passed to our team, the comment from everyone was, 'Oh, yeah? So he sez.'"

Leaside won the opener of the best-of-three series, 12–7. "Ronnie Taylor grew steadily better as the game went on, allowing 8 hits, striking out 10 and walking but 2," Kronk wrote in the booklet. "He set the losers down in order in the last two frames. Dumbo Caffery was the big hitter for Leaside with 4 saftie [sic] including a homer with 3 on in the fourth."

Leaside won the second game and the title, 12–4. Sez we!

Advancing to the Ontario Baseball Association playoffs on September 7, Taylor shut out Mimico, 7–0, on four hits and 12 Ks. Leaside won the second game, 6–0, on a Kennedy no-hitter (Taylor had two hits and a sacrifice fly), and beat Kirchener in a three-game semi, whereupon the bus to the finals in Hamilton stalled in Humber. "I had visions of hiring taxis to take us to Hamilton," Kronk wrote. "Davy Green's father, after tinkering with the starter, finally got it going; and it did not stop until we got to the ball park in Hamilton."

Despite facing bigger players on the Hamilton team and "particularly bad umpiring," Leaside and Kennedy won the opener 5–3. "It was a happy team that left for Leaside. Quite a few parents were on the trip, so a stop was made for foot-long hot dogs on the highway. "A sing songled by Phil [Stein] and featuring a continuous chorus of Good Night Irene was not enjoyed by all the listeners." Kennedy also won the final of the home-and-home series, 6–3, with Taylor going 2-for-3.

Leaside now qualified for the TMBA finals on October 21 against Ottawa. The team took a train to the national capital, toured Parliament and saw a hockey game. Then the Cubs beat the Ottawa East Flyers, 4–1, behind Kennedy. "Ron Taylor continued his terrific hitting in the play-downs by getting three sol-

id safeties and was robbed of a fourth on a sensational catch by
Hutchins, Flyer short-fielder."

The finale, back at Talbot Park on October 28, was switched
to a softball diamond when the field was too wet. Kennedy set
down Ottawa, 9–4. Now, what have you noted about Taylor's
play? Yes, he was the number two pitcher and a good-hitting out-
~~fielder, but th~~

~~y ~~Park], who coached Taylor for the 1954
Metropolitan Motors, said later. "He's a low-ball pitcher and has
good control with his fastball. He also had a pretty good curve
and slider when he was here."

Later Roncetti was elected to the Canadian Baseball Hall of
Fame. "Ron told me things about pitching then that I'm still hearing from coaches in the big leagues," says Taylor, who felt Roncetti improved the youngster's self-worth at a tender age where he
might have doubted it. That's not all Roncetti did for his young
charge. Roncetti owned a billiard parlor and turned Taylor into
a successful hustler "when some New Yorker would think he'd
take a few quick bucks from some Canadian," Taylor confided to
Bob Elliott, author of *The Northern Game: Baseball The Canadian Way.*

Thanks to Roncetti's influence with the Toronto Maple Leafs
Triple-A team, Taylor had days when he would unload bunker oil
from tankers at Toronto's harbor, pitch 30–45 minutes of batting
practice for the Leafs and play for the Metropolitan Motors Club
in a 21-and-under league (talk about multi-tasking!). It was just
a matter of time before Chester Dies, the Cleveland scout who
started bird-dogging Taylor when the lad was 13, convinced him
to take that train ride to Cleveland.

Let's not overlook other events in his life. Ron was already
a math, chemistry and physics whiz who had as many friends

among the scholars as the athletes at North Toronto Collegiate Institute, a good public school. No American-style high school jock/chick magnet/study slacker for him; he worked hard and was barely aware that girls existed. "I think I took out a couple of girls in grade school. I was pretty good [at studies and sports] because there were no distractions. I always had that will: I wanted to be an engineer and play big-league baseball."

In addition to his other activities, Taylor was an airman with the Royal Canadian Air Force (Auxiliary 411) at ages 16–18 and worked as an airframe technician. At the time he took that fateful train trip to Cleveland, Taylor worked as an airframe technician on de Havilland Vampire jets, with "3,000 pounds of static thrust" from its Goblin engine. Unlike his brother-in-law Bruce Mitchell, he'd never get to pilot a plane.

The scene of a kid arriving in the minor leagues is popularized in myth: the young hayseed, scared stiff, thumbing a ride to the training camp. It wasn't that way for Ron Taylor when he arrived in Daytona Beach, Florida in March of 1956. "The airport was right next to the training camp," he says. "It was just a question of someone giving me a ride. I wasn't scared stiff because I'd worked out with major leaguers and played in Toronto with guys four or five years older than I was. I had no fear at all. I knew I'd be a big-league ballplayer from day one. I wouldn't have dropped out of Grade 13 if I didn't have that confidence."

Early in the season, Ron and a first baseman collided, injuring Taylor's back. He got over it quickly, and the injury lay dormant for a decade. Taylor loved the bus trips around Florida, during which he, as inconspicuously as possible, studied for the exams he'd put off, concentrating mostly on math and physics. "As far as anyone knew, I could have been reading the paper," he says.

"We were a bunch of 18-and-19-year-olds, and we had a great manager in Hank Majeski. He treated us all as if we were his kids, which we needed." When Taylor went 17–11 and convinced the Indians to let him skip future spring trainings, he embarked on a journey with no precedent in baseball or engineering. But first he and some buddies took a side trip to New York City and met a very interesting man. When they entered Toots Shor's, a popular watering spot for celebrities, they were introduced to one Ernest Hemingway, who greeted them cordially. "We had studied him in high school," Taylor said. "I was in awe."

In the University of Toronto's compressed four-year curriculum, Taylor primarily studied the design and function of electrical machines and transmissions. He was popular among his fellow

pressed that there were two things he did so well.

Taylor had to work harder for acceptance when he arrived at his subsequent minor league stops after the university classes ended in late April. The initial feeling was, "Here's that Canadian again," Taylor says. "I said, 'One of you is leaving, because I'm staying.' I was really cocky. I didn't have many friends at first." Having run every day and thrown every other day during the school year, Taylor made a quick transition from student to thrower and broke down his teammates' resistance.

Taylor routinely moved into the rotation after a week or two. Setting an example, he didn't complain about being boarded in cheap hotels or with families and didn't grouse about mind-numbing bus trips like the 600-mile journey from Minot, North Dakota, to Eau Claire, Wisconsin. "I had a great summer job for a student," he says.

"There's no such thing as a minor-league baseball career," Taylor told Canadian Boy magazine's Norman Brown. "There's no future there. Maybe you can make a good living in Triple-A, but not below that. And when you're young, you should be building a career for yourself. So it's tough to stay in minor-league ball when you could be doing something else. The minors are not a money-making proposition at all, but a training ground for young players. The average minor leaguer is about 20 or 21 and he gets out of baseball in a few years if he can't make it to the major leagues."

Taylor figured that because of his foreshortened minor-league seasons he should allow five years just to reach Triple-A. But succeeding at every level gave him hope. Majeski, his manager for the Daytona Beach Islanders in 1956, told Taylor he had one of the best arms of anyone he'd seen in the minors. With the Class-A Fargo-Moorhead ND Twins in 1957, he threw five shutouts, enough that farm director Hoot Evers flew out to see him. With the Minot ND Ducks, another Class-A Northern League team, in 1958, he was one of the circuit's leading pitchers, right up there with future major-leaguers Gaylord Perry and Bo Belinski. With Double-A Reading PA in 1959, he routinely went nine innings and threw three scoreless ones in the league All-Star Game. He had another successful year with Reading the following season.

"I was always able to flip over from student to ballplayer," Taylor recalls. "Getting ready for spring training, I'd draw a box on a brick wall and throw high and tight, low and away." Sometimes he'd pitch to his best friend, the late Peter Biggs, at least as long as Biggs's catching hand held up to Taylor's fastballs. After graduation from the University of Toronto in 1961, Taylor convinced the Indians' Evers to use him in the rotation at Triple-A Salt Lake City and invited him to the spring training the following season.

The Salt Lake season was Taylor's first taste of adversity. Because he'd been studying for and taking final exams at the university, he skipped some workouts and needed more time to get into shape. In a league with future major-league pitchers like Perry, Herb Score and Sam McDowell, not to mention plenty of good hitters, Taylor wasn't going nine innings often and started slowly. But the Indians didn't regret inviting him to spring training the next year.

Breathless and comma-less, the 1962 Indians Sketchbook reported, "His 8–9 mark at Salt Lake City last season was not outstanding but he did display enough ability and poise [Taylor finished the season strongly] to warrant being invited to Tucson this spring where he was impressive. He has a live fastball and boundless confidence in himself and in his ability to pitch himself out of trouble." Indians' manager Mel McGaha said, "The tip-off on

Ron is that even though he reported late—sometimes by as much as two months—he always caught up with other pitchers on his team in innings pitched. When I managed Toronto [1960], Ron used to come out here and pitch batting practice between classes. I'm very impressed with him."

So impressed that McGaha started Taylor on April 11 in the

quette, once described in the Boston Globe as "the classy curver from Medford." Taylor even broke up Monbo's no-hitter with a single in the sixth inning and got another single for half the Indians' hits. In the 12th inning of a scoreless game, Boston's Carl Yastrzemski led off with a triple on a fly misjudged by centerfielder Ty Cline. After intentionally walking the next two batters, Taylor yielded a game-ending grand slam to Carroll Hardy. His totals: 11 innings, 10 hits, four earned runs, three walks, five strikeouts. Gordon Cobbledick, sports editor of the Cleveland Plain Dealer, called Taylor's outing "one of the most remarkable rookie pitching performances in all baseball history."

"Everybody said it was a tough game to lose, but I wasn't disappointed," Taylor said. "I felt very satisfied that I was able to pitch so well for so long in my very first game."

Thirteen days later Taylor beat Dean Chance (Cline drove in the winning run). Taylor's success, then and for the remainder of his career, depended on two things: good health and keeping the ball low. In a typical progression, he would waste a pitch up and in, driving the batter back, before throwing several sinkers or sliders in the lowest and farthest reaches of the strike zone where the batter could do least damage. As Taylor's future St. Louis teammate Curt Simmons explained to author David Halberstam, pitchers keep the ball low because God attached arms to the shoulders, not hips. High pitches in the strike zone, therefore, were easier for batters to reach.

Is pitching strategy really this simple? There are some other factors like scouting reports on hitter's weaknesses, the game situation, the runners and pitching to location rather than trying to strike hitters out; but there's a danger of what ballplayers call "paralysis through analysis." Asked if baseball was more mental than physical, Jim Lonborg, who won a Cy Young Award with the 1967 Red Sox, said, "If it was, I'd be soaking my head in ice, not my arm."

At this point, Taylor lacked the focus and pitch location to stay in the majors. After some bad outings, he was demoted to Jacksonville in May with a 2–2 record and a 5.94 ERA.

"I find baseball and engineering equally exciting," Taylor told Cobbledick's colleague Hall Lebovitz after the demotion. "Ever since I was a small boy, I've had two ambitions: to be a ballplayer and an engineer. I know I can make good in the latter field. My school work proved it. But I have to find out if I can make good in baseball. There would be an awful vacuum in my life if I quit now.

"Believe me, I'm not in baseball for the money. If that was my main goal, I'd have turned to engineering immediately. Right now, the challenge of the big leagues is foremost in my mind. Can I make it here? I'm giving myself a year to find out."

Taylor headed south with McGaha's words in his mind. "[He] said that a ballplayer should try to be mentally alert and physically relaxed. That way, you're not physically tight, but you're ready to make the moves when you have to. For instance, if a pitcher is physically tense, he grips the ball too tightly and can't throw a good fastball."

Growing stronger, improving his control, Taylor went 12–4, with a 2.66 ERA (second best in the league), 10 complete games, 114 strikeouts and only 36 walks in 180 innings. "You ain't got nothing on the ball but your hand, Taylor," Sparky Anderson, then a second baseman, later a Hall of Fame manager, barked at him. "He was serious," says Taylor. "I think he was angry because he couldn't hit me. We became good friends after that."

After Jacksonville won the International League pennant, Taylor was 0–2, but with a 1.17 ERA, in the playoff loss to the Atlanta Crackers, a St. Louis farm team. His future Cardinal teammate Ray Sadecki won both games. Tim McCarver, who caught for the Crackers, described Taylor as "lights out that season." Third baseman Mike de la Hoz nicknamed him "Steely," as in Man of

side me when I was warming up in the bullpen," Taylor said. "I didn't know who he was, and he left before the game started. A week later one of the coaches on my team said, 'I have some good news for you. There's a good chance you'll be moving on.'"

Keane had told the Cardinals' general manager Bing Devine that he wanted Taylor on the team because he was "not afraid of the bat." On December 15, 1962, the Cardinals traded first baseman Fred Whitfield to the Indians for Taylor and infielder Jack Kubiszyn. Whitfield was a major crowd pleaser and an explosive hitter, but the Cardinals were convinced they were getting something better.

The encomiums poured in. Bing Devine, the Cardinals' general manager, said Taylor had a chance to become the team's number four starter. "Taylor is a great competitor who has a loose delivery, not herky-jerky, that has enabled him to pitch often," Schultz explained. "He has a good slider, a pretty good fast ball and a fair curve.

"The important thing is that he keeps the ball low, and he's always around the plate."

Taylor went from a losing club to a winning one. With a little luck and a lot of pluck, he was going to make it bigtime.

The Cards' Ace In the Hole

When Taylor joined St. Louis in 1963, the Cardinals were climbing out of a deep hole. They hadn't won a pennant in 17 years. By failing to integrate as fast as other teams in the National League, the Cardinals didn't access the most promising new player pool in professional sports. Things began to change when August A. Busch, Jr. bought the team in 1953 and famously asked where all the black players were. By 1963 the team had some African-American stars like right-hander Bob Gibson, center fielder Curt Flood and first baseman Bill White. Another black player, base-stealing whiz Lou Brock, would join the club the following season. Meanwhile, Red Schoendienst and Stan Musial were finishing their careers en route to Cooperstown, where Gibson and Brock would join them in the Hall of Fame. The '63 Cardinals were a story of baseball history retiring and baseball history abuilding.

Though he was technically still a rookie, Taylor was paid $10,000, or $4,000 over the rookie minimum, and says he suffered none of the hazing so common in baseball. "The older players—White, [Dick] Groat, [Ken] Boyer—were nice to me. It was a team effort, pulling for your teammate."

Taylor tried to fit in as inconspicuously as he could, and he substantially succeeded. About the only thing his teammates noticed about his personal style was that he was wearing contact lenses at a time when most sight-impaired players wore glasses. Tim McCarver called him "Blinky."

"His quiet and reserved personality made him a contrast from a clubhouse full of future broadcasters," Maxwell Kates wrote in a bio prepared for a University of Nebraska Press book on the 1964 Cardinals.

"I had a terrible spring," Taylor remembers. "I was trying to steer the ball instead of throwing it. I was worried. One day after I got lit up, Branch Rickey, who was sitting behind the dugout, said, 'Come over here.' I came over, expecting the worst. 'You're going to be fine, kid,' he said. I was pressing, not relaxing; and he relaxed me." It may have been the last useful advice Rickey, who had integrated the majors with Jackie Robinson but was finishing his career as a cranky senior consultant to the Cardinals, would make in baseball. He died the next year.

Taylor's sinker-slider style succeeded immediately. There was just one disappointment for him. The Cardinals had traded relievers Lindy McDaniel to the Cubs a year earlier and Bobby Shantz

Taylor finished the season by winning nine, saving 11 (with little fanfare since the save statistic still didn't exist officially until 1969) and recording a 2.84 ERA in 54 appearances. In perhaps his highlight outing, on September 14, he entered a game with no outs and runners on first and third in the ninth to protect a 3–2 lead, and retired the side on a foul out, a strikeout and a ground ball. Ray Culp of the Phillies, who was 14–10 as a starter, won *The Sporting News* Rookie Pitcher of the Year; it's hard to find anyone else with stats to match Taylor's. His save total might not seem like much, but this was in an era when starters wanted to finish, and 26.7% did in 1963. Taylor tied for seventh in the National League in saves and 10th in appearances. Again, saves were unofficial and unlisted at the time.

If his personal style was understated, his approach to pitching made people take notice. He could warm up using very few pitches. "Ron was a nervous, maniacally fast worker, like a tiger in a cage," McCarver said. In a more recent interview, McCarver said, "If you knew Ron Taylor, you knew he was a man of few words when he worked. In 1963, I went out to the mound; and he said, 'Keep your ass behind home plate.' At the end of the inning, we had a confrontation in the dugout. I was waiting for him to hit me, and I was going to hit him back. He said, 'You were showing *me* up.' I said, 'You were showing *me* up'" They never did come to blows.

Typical of the high standard Taylor set for himself, he says he helped cost the Cardinals the pennant with his pitching on September 18. Appearing with two outs in the eighth and a 5–4 lead over the Dodgers, he got out of the inning but yielded a homer in the ninth to Dick Nen, a rookie making his major league debut. Taylor was pinch-hit for in the Cardinal ninth, and the Dodgers won in 13 innings, 6–5. The Cardinals finished fully six games behind LA in second place, so you might say Taylor was tough on himself.

He was pitching from a three-quarters motion with his index and middle fingers together on the ball between the seams and slightly to the right of center. He'd squeeze harder on his middle finger and turn his wrist to the right on his slider, producing a right-to-left route to the plate ideally ending in a drop over the outside corner to right-handed batters. To throw a sinker—really a sinking fastball—he'd squeeze the index finger and twist the wrist slightly to the left. "It's the same as an airplane wing; it's a pressure difference. The airplane wing has the same rotation as the pitch."

Between seasons Taylor was working as an engineer for a Chicago plant owned by an American company with some Canadian employees called Interlake Steel. "I would run wind sprints and throw against walls after work. One night I was out running around midnight and a policeman stopped me and put me up against a car with my legs spread. He thought I'd committed a crime and was escaping. "What are you doing?' he said.

"'I'm getting in shape for spring training.'

"'Let me see your identification.' I had my birth certificate and residence paper.

"'Now let me get this straight. Why are you running?'

"'To get into shape. I'm a major league player.'

"'Let me get this straight. You're a major-league player. You're in Chicago and living in Canada. Did you miss a turn somewhere? Don't ever run outside again. Run in a gym.'"

For the 1964 season, the Cardinals asked Taylor to develop an overhand curve between seasons, a bad idea for someone who succeeded on keeping pitches low. Early in the 1964 season, he couldn't get his pitches down. His first outing was hardly auspicious, when he surrendered a two-run homer to the Dodgers' Frank Howard on April 14. Three days later Taylor walked in the winning run. After mopping up a 7–1 loss, he walked the only two batters he faced, and both scored the last runs of a 7–5 loss. By the June 15 trading deadline, Taylor was 0–1, with a 5.80 ERA

last 29 games. Brock stole 33 bases, hit .348 over 103 games and led the Cardinals to the pennant. And fortunately, Busch stuck with his manager. "Keane was a gentleman, a family man who cared for people—a good fit for St. Louis," Taylor says.

The subject of team "chemistry" is a controversial one in baseball. Some say teams don't have to get along to win big: just look at the A's of the early Seventies and the Yankees later in the decade. Others point to the seven free agents the 2013 Red Sox signed who were as well known for their clubhouse presence as on-field prowess. For St. Louis, a team with a proud history, players who don't preen and fans who are good-natured and fair-minded, chemistry counts. There was a calm cool about the 1964 Cardinals. They were steeped in fundamentals and knew that over a long season you don't get too high when things are going well, or too low when they're going poorly. Taylor shared an apartment with Dal Maxvill and Charlie James, who were also trained as electrical engineers. Race relations were better than on most teams, as per witness the daily bridge competition that matched Bill White (black) and Ken Boyer (white) against Bob Gibson (black) and Dick Groat (white). The black players felt Keane supported them.

Over the course of a long season with more bumps than a dirt country road, humor can do much for team chemistry. Taylor refers to Bob Uecker, a second-string catcher who later became a broadcaster, actor, comedian and pitchman, as "the best teammate you could ever have." In his book *October 1964*, David Halberstam underscored Uecker's hilarious influence on the club:

"Uecker pitched batting practice every day, and in time he created the Uecker League, of which he was the commissioner, umpire, and scorekeeper. There were two teams of five pitchers each in the Uecker League [one managed by Sadecki, the other by Taylor]. There was a draft among the pitchers, and they chose sides, and when the pitchers took batting practice at home (they did not get batting practice on the road), Uecker would stand on the mound and decide whether a player had gotten a hit. All ground balls and pop-ups were outs. If there were runners on base, he decided how far they advanced on a play. The pitchers themselves did the scoring and kept their batting averages. On occasion there were trades from one team to the other. Once Taylor, one of the bullpen pitchers, batted out of turn [Uecker remembers that it was a member of Taylor's team]. A protest was immediately lodged. Uecker demanded to see the scorecard, but before he could look at it, Taylor ate it."

Sadecki filed a protest. A close season was on the line and the possibility of a playoff lingered. "So I had to follow him [Taylor] around for a couple of days, sort of waiting and watching, hoping he'd pass the thing so I could make some kind of ruling," Uecker told Bob Cairns, the author of *Pen Men: Baseball's Greatest Stories Told by the Men Who Brought the Game Relief*. "But the protest went for naught. I was never fortunate enough to be at the right place at the right time. He must have passed it but I wasn't there to make the call."

Keeping their spirits up and their humor intact, the Cardinals rebounded swiftly over the second half-season. Taylor did his part, getting the ball down, going 7–1 in 21 games. He led the Cardinals with 63 appearances—a team record at the time—while winning eight and saving six unofficially. In one memorable game, on June 18, he reported to preserve a one-run lead over the Giants with one out and runners on first and second in the ninth, and proceeded to strike out Willie Mays and get Orlando Cepeda to foul out.

But Keane wanted someone who could pitch every day. No one can pitch more often than a knuckleballer because the pitch taxes the arm less than other deliveries. So 37-year-old knuckleballer Barney Schultz, back from his latest minor-league stint on July 31, became the team's go-to closer most of the time and pitched in 30 of the last 59 games. It was hard to argue with his

on ice, but the celebration was as weird and indecipherable as "Hotel California." Poor Bing Devine walked in. Before being fired, he had built the Cardinals into contenders over the years and traded for useful right-hander Roger Craig and Brock. In fact, Devine would be voted baseball's executive of the year. But he'd also been fired. Devine didn't know how to act toward the players, and vice-versa. Meanwhile, Bob Uecker danced nude, among broken glass from a broken bottle, to the World-War-Two song, "Pass the Biscuits, Miranda." After partying in their clubhouse, the Cardinals attended a victory celebration at Stan Musial's restaurant. Then something really strange happened that Tim McCarver described in *We Played the Game: 65 Players Remember Baseball's Greatest Era, 1947–64*, edited by Danny Peary. "We noticed that Ron Taylor was missing, and we started asking 'Where's [Ronnie?']...A guard went back to the stadium and found him in his uniform, passed out under his dress clothes with his feet out. He had hyperventilated. The guard put him under the shower and revived him and he joined us at the party. It was a strange day." [Taylor told Elliott, "I was relaxing."]

If Taylor was something of an overlooked player as the World Series started, he was one of its largely unsung heroes by the time it ended. Let's set the scene. The Cardinals managed a split of the first two games in St. Louis, but when the Series shifted to New York, Mickey Mantle hit a walk-off homer to win Game Three.

With two more wins at home, the Yankees could win the Series. There was a sense of inevitability. Only three St. Louis players had Series experience, while the Yankees were playing in their fifth straight Series and 15th in the last 18 years. The wind was blowing out toward the right-field fence 296 feet from home, duck soup for Yankee sluggers like Mantle and Roger Maris. The Cardinals, by contrast, were struggling at the plate: Curt Flood (2-for-14); Lou Brock (2-for-13); Ken Boyer (1-for-11); Bill White (1-for-11); and Dal Maxvill (2-for-7); with Mike Shannon (4-for-11) and Tim McCarver (4-for-9) the surprising batting leaders. It hardly seemed important that Yankee left-hander Whitey Ford needed a day off to recover from a heel injury; Al Downing would do fine.

Sure enough, the Cardinals were heading quickly for what seemed a third loss. Ray Sadecki allowed the four Yankees he faced to reach base, and two of them to score. A throwing error by third baseman Ken Boyer, which blew a rundown when Phil Linz was trapped between second and third, proved costly. How often do your first four hitters reach base and you lose?

With one out and a runner on third, Keane called on Craig, a sad-faced North Carolinian who could do a great hillbilly imitation. Craig had the face of a hound but the mind of a fox. As a Met, he had lost 24 games in 1962 and 22 in 1963; but he'd also thrown 27 complete games. With tongue only partly inserted in cheek, Craig explained his skill to the Dodgers' Don Drysdale when they were paired on the dais at a dinner following the 1962 season. How many games had Drysdale won, Craig asked him.

"Twenty-five."

"And how many games did your team win?"

"One hundred and three."

"Well, Don, I guess I'm more valuable to the Mets than you are to the Dodgers because I won 10 games this year, whereas the Mets won only 40 and that's a larger percentage of the team's victories than you had."

When Craig was traded to the Cardinals, Hall of Famer Ralph Kiner, then a Mets announcer, said he might mean a pennant in St. Louis. "He's a great competitor and he gives the Cards a great middle-relief pitcher or a starter," Kiner said. "He pitches hard every time he's out there."

A pitcher with several speeds that could be used with several different deliveries, Craig won seven, saved five and threw $7^2/_3$ shutout innings in a key game on September 27. And he was smart enough that he'd go on to manage the San Francisco Giants to two division titles and one pennant later in his life, punctuating his delight with a catchy phrase, "Hum, baby!"

embarrassed lug on the cheek. But there was nothing funny about his pitching. After giving up Elston Howard's run-scoring single to make it 3–0, Yankees, Craig allowed one more hit and no more scoring while striking out eight batters over $4^2/_3$ innings. He was not only outpitching the Yankee hitters but also outthinking their baserunners. When he threw to Groat to pick off off Mickey Mantle with two out and runners on first and second in the third, Mantle passed Craig and snarled, "You son of a bitch. You show me up in front of 40 million people."

In the Cardinal sixth, with the Yankees still ahead, 3–0, and Downing having allowed just one bloop single, Carl Warwick batted for Craig and got his third pinch-hitting base hit of the Fall Classic to tie a Series record. Curt Flood singled him to second, and Brock flied out. Then Dick Groat hit a ground ball to second baseman Bobby Richardson. This surely was it. Using a cherished baseball mainstay, the Yankees would cool the Cardinals' fire and snuff out their chances with a double play. As the late journalist Alistair Cooke put it, "Next to a triple play, baseball's double play is the most exciting and graceful thing in sports."

But as the normally slick-fielding Richardson fielded Groat's potential inning-ender, he couldn't get the ball out of his glove. By the time Richardson made a gloved-hand flip to second, shortstop Phil Linz had passed the base and couldn't handle the throw.

Thanks to Richardson's error, the bases were loaded. Ken Boyer stepped in. Behind the plate, Elston Howard called for a fastball, and Al Downing shook him off. Boyer, the first-inning fielding blunderer, set himself for a Downing changeup, got one and hit a line shot down the left-field line. "It could be; it may be; it's a home run," Harry Caray said on the national radio broadcast. The drive had cleared the fence five or six feet in fair territory. It was only the ninth grand slam—Caray and his broadcast mate, Curt Gowdy, called it a "grand slammer"—in Series history. Suddenly, the Cardinals led, 4–3. "It doesn't take long to go from bum to hero, hero to bum," Caray said.

Schultz had already pitched in the first three games, twice ineffectively; and it was too early in the game for him, anyway. So Keane called on a future team doctor to stop of the bleeding. Taylor, who had been heckled by Yankee fans while warming up in the bullpen down the left-field line, took over in the bottom of the sixth. The lineup he faced was no Murderers Row, but there wasn't a pit stop in it, either. Heeding Boyer's advice to "Lay off the cute stuff…just fire the ball," and using the "hazy, checkered background" batters saw as they looked toward the mound, according to *Sports Illustrated*, Taylor challenged the Yankees with his best sinkers and sliders, as well as a few curves. He promptly got Howard on a grounder to first. Switch-hitting Tom Tresh came up batting left-handed. "This is the type of left-handed batter who gave Taylor trouble during the season," Caray, who called the Cardinals games, said. Tresh missed a good curveball inside and struck out swinging on a fastball. Joe Pepitone—a "good pull-hitter, extremely dangerous in this park"—grounded to Maxvill at second.

The Cardinals were through scoring. All Taylor had to do was shut down Mantle, Maris and the other guys. In the seventh, Boyer's brother Clete fouled to first; pinch hitter John Blanchard flied to center and Phil Linz, trying to bunt, grounded to third. An inning later, Taylor faced his toughest batters. Richardson grounded to short. Maris ripped a hard grounder up the middle but Taylor deflected it to shortstop Dick Groat, who had been cheating to his left, and Groat made a great stab and threw in time to first.

Mantle, Taylor felt, was a special case. "I didn't want to give him anything too good," he said later. "I didn't want him to pull the ball into those inviting right-field seats." Especially with the wind blowing out. Mantle blew on his hands and stepped in. Taking a full windup, with his right foot on the left side of the rubber, Taylor worked deliberately, pausing noticeably between pitches.

the 66,312 fans pleading in vain for a Yankees rally, Taylor made their ninth-inning batters look laughable. Tresh tried to bunt, but Taylor threw him out. Pepitone and Clete Boyer could only ground to first. No one got the ball out of the infield, and that was typical of Taylor's no-hit afternoon. Of the 12 batters he retired, one flied to center; one fouled to the first baseman; two struck out; and eight grounded out. In one of the virtuoso performances of World Series history, Taylor threw only 36 pitches over four innings, 27 of them for strikes. Four of the nine balls were served ever so carefully to Mantle. Taylor had McCarver set up over the outside corner against left-handed hitters; he hit that exact spot consistently, as McCarver said afterward.

"His control was as perfect as any time I ever caught him," McCarver said recently. And that wasn't all. "Usually balls that are thrown straight are not heavy balls. In other words, they don't sink quickly. But his forearms were strong, and he threw a straight, heavy fastball [that did sink]. It tore my left [glove] hand up because the late movement made it difficult to catch. I couldn't decipher it. If I couldn't, the hitters certainly couldn't."

Craig got the win; Taylor the save. "It was the greatest thrill of my life to help win the game," Taylor said.

"Sitting here years later, I can still remember every pitch I threw," Taylor said. "It was an unbelievable existential experience."

Craig and Taylor had thrown a two-hitter over $8^2/_3$ innings. Keane said, "That has to be the finest relief work we've had. It couldn't be improved upon. Craig and Taylor were splendid."

Halberstam called Game Four "the crucial game of the 1964 World Series." Writers swarmed over Craig and Taylor in the Cardinal clubhouse. "It's the first time in the Series anyone has been talking to us," Taylor said in the ghostwritten column he did on the Series for the Toronto Star. When a writer apologized for asking him what he'd just said in the noisy room, he said, "Gee, I'm enjoying it. Nothing like this ever happened to me before."

Oh, Taylor was good copy. Asked if he was related to E.P. Taylor, owner of the racehorse Northern Dancer, he replied, "But I'm not. He's the wealthy one." Pressed for more information about himself, Taylor ad-libbed, "Put it this way: I'm the first right-handed Canadian who ever relieved in the World Series in New York on a Sunday."

Despite Boyer's insistence, with his arms around Craig and Taylor, that "Those are the guys who won the game," the wire services stories published around the country in the following day's papers concentrated primarily on home-run guy Boyer and secondarily on Mets-loser-turned-Card-winner Craig, who was remembered for a Series win when he pitched for the Dodgers. Where were the "Introducing Ron Taylor" stories?

In any case, he quickly receded from view. After Tim McCarver's 10th-inning homer won Game Five, 5–2, Taylor got Jim Bouton, the only batter he faced, to hit into a double play in Sadecki's 8–3 Game-Six loss. Then Series MVP Gibson, making his third start in eight days, held on to win the finale despite two ninth-inning homers, 7–5. (Taylor and Ray Sadecki were warming up in the bullpen at game's end.) The other anointed Series hero, McCarver, played every inning and batted .478. "Sat my way through it," Uecker, ever the loyal bench-warmer, said. "Called it from the bullpen. Yankee fans threw garbage at us, and I picked it up and threw it back."

The enormity of Taylor's dike-stopping work in Game Four was only evident in the rear-view mirror. "You know, when you talk about the greatest pitching performances of the Series, that really is a game that never gets its due," outfielder Mike Shannon told Bob Elliott of the Toronto Sun. "Roger gave up two singles in 4²/₃ innings, and Doc held them hitless for four innings. They shut down that powerful Yankee club." Without that win, Shannon thought, the Series might not have returned to St. Louis.

Richardson's critical error that led to four Cardinals runs in Game Four. Ken B____'s h____ d____ li f d

_____ __ ____ ____ ____ ____ ____ ____ __ Game Four they might have won easily.

As it was, the Cardinals' victory represented a paradigm shift in the baseball world. The Yankee hegemony that had lasted since the 1920s was over when they lost their second straight Series for the first time in 42 years: the fabled Bronx Bombers wouldn't play in another Series for 12 years. The new baseball world, now represented by the diversified Cardinals, had passed them by. They paid the price for integrating late (1955) and ignoring the talent in the Caribbean.

Now, the Yankees faced a team and league that celebrated the recruitment of top blacks and Latinos. (This was actually more style than substance, since the National League played seven full seasons before more than half of its clubs were integrated. But the image of integration may have made the league more attractive to the best minority players.) The Cardinals routinely started three blacks, Curt Flood, Lou Brock and Bill White, and one Hispanic, Julián Javier. (A bruised hip limited Javier to one pinch-running appearance in the World Series.) Gibson, an African-American, was one of the league's best pitchers; and the Cuban lefthander Mike Cuellar was also on the team. The Yankees started one black, Elston Howard; had a black pitcher, Downing; a substitute outfielder, the Panamanian Hector Lopez; and a Cuban pitcher, Pedro Ramos, who saved seven games by the unofficial pre-1969 standard down the stretch but joined the team after September 1 and wasn't eligible for the World Series. In the 1950s and 1960s, the National League had 15 blacks and Hispanics of a possible 20 Most Valuable Players; the Americans three. Although the American League held its own in the World Series, beginning in 1964 the Nationals won 18 of 19 All-Star Games. For their part, the Cardinals are still the only one of the original eight National League teams to hold a Series edge (3–2) over the Yankees.

Following the 1964 season the majors would initiate a draft of players signing their first contracts that would invalidate the winning tradition the Yankees would otherwise have tempted them with in an open market. Ron Taylor and his teammates stood at the crossroads of baseball history.

Canadians remember their heroes and celebrate them to beat the band. Speaking at the Metropolitan Toronto Amateur Baseball Association dinner following the '64 Series, Taylor showed his quick wit in answer to questions:

Q.—What's the best pitch to throw Mickey Mantle?

A.—A ball.

Q.—How many homers have you hit?

A.—Just one, and it was foul by a foot.

Q.—Who's the best hitter you've ever faced?

A.—I make them all look good. Mantle is the best—and oh, yes, Willie Mays. He's pretty good too.

Q.—What kind of a fellow is Stan Musial?

A.—Just tremendous, although we usually went different ways after a game. Stan would go to the bank, and I'd go to the finance company.

Q.—Who's the easiest player to get out?

A.—Another pitcher.

Taylor was also feted by the Leaside Baseball Association. The scroll he received read in part: "For the Honour you have brought to the town of Leaside, we are truly grateful." Taylor replied. "It is I who am grateful to the town of Leaside for giving me the opportunity to play organized baseball." He got a standing ovation.

To grasp what happened next in Taylor's career, it's necessary to understand the nature of our national pastime. Baseball is nothing if not a yo-yo sport: up one minute, down the next. Its skills are so refined that they can be gained and lost in a trice. Some of the best baseball writing traces the game's vicissitudes.

Johnette Howard in *Sports Illustrated*: "Baseball is the sport that cackles back at can't miss kids. Baseball humbles every player sooner or later. Baseball confers greatness stingily, in its own

Si tendre	So tender
Si désespéré	So desperate
Cet amour	This love
Beau comme le jour	Beautiful like the day
Et mauvais comme le temps	And bad like the weather
Quand le temps est mauvais	When the weather is bad

That's baseball. April is the cruelest month for ballplayers, breeding false hopes all too quickly quashed. But we digress.

Halfway through the 1965 season, the seventh-place Cardinals acquired Hal Woodeschick in a trade that sent Taylor and Mike Cuellar to the ninth-place Houston Colt .45s. The Houstons were slightly better than the Mets but much less interesting, even though they played in the new Astrodome, hyped as "the eighth wonder of the world." Though he'd been dealt to baseball's Valley of Ashes, Taylor kept his humor intact. "Yep, I've been here before," he told Hal Lundgren of the *Houston Post*. "You might call me an old Domer."

He soon felt like an old-timer. Quick- and high-bouncing artificial turf was unsuited to low-ball pitchers, and Taylor was used to starting and short relief, not the middle relief and mop-up Houston eventually gave him over 57 appearances. "I felt I wasn't used properly," Taylor told Maury Allen of the *New York Post*.

Taylor stumbled through the 1965 season, depressed, wondering if he had any future in baseball. That wasn't the only problem. In the spring of 1966, he bent over to pick up a ball, felt back pain and couldn't straighten up. The Daytona Beach injury from 10 years earlier was flaring up again. "I had a lumbosacral spine strain in the lower back, and I tried to play through it," Taylor says. He was in such discomfort that when the trainer shut him down and insisted on a medical examination, he had to stand during an entire flight back to Houston, airline regulations be damned.

"He was in traction at Houston Methodist Hospital, where I was a resident," Don Patrick, a retired neurosurgeon Ron's age, says. "The orthopedist who was in change of him stopped me in the hall and said, 'There's a baseball player, but he's different. He's an intellectual!'

"I stopped by his room. Dadgum, he was smart! He knew about philosophy and history, and he was interested in medicine. He said, 'I've got this trouble. You're a neurosurgeon. Why don't you tell me about the back?' He wanted to see a skeleton and know how the muscles and nerves worked. He was thirsty about information, and he could remember it.

"I'd been around athletes before, because I ran track for three seasons at Texas A & I. I dressed with football, baseball and basketball players; and they were about pushing people around. I was 6'3", 150 pounds and easy to push around. We didn't have many intellectuals who were athletes. In fact, the athletes looked down on them. This guy was different."

For his part, Patrick did 400 brain operations at the legendary 24th Evacuation Hospital in Vietnam, won a Bronze Star, got a law degree, practiced medico-legal and elder law, and later earned a Master's in music by writing his thesis about the 16th century violinist Biaggi Marini. He found a kindred spirit in Taylor. They became lifelong friends, and Patrick has visited Taylor in New York and Toronto. "Next to marrying my second wife, the smartest thing I ever did was making the connection with Ron," says Patrick, from whom we'll be hearing more later.

Back before there were radiographic diagnoses, the doctors at Methodist gave Taylor an eX-ray and a myelogram, the latter an X-ray in which a needle injects dye between the bones to check for infections, tumors, herniated discs, arthritis and other causes of pain in the lower spine. The dye never leaves the body. Myelograms have largely been replaced by CT and MRI scans, which

didn't help his back.

"When athletes come off AstroTurf, they're like arthritics," Jim Parkes, former Mets' physician, told Dan Schlossberg, author of *The Baseball Catalogue.*

"Their ankles hurt, their shins hurt, their backs hurt. Astroturf is like concrete; there's no give."

"Playing on Astroturf didn't help," Taylor says. "I was ready for a soft surface."

In the spring of 1967, Houston demoted Taylor to its Triple-A Oklahoma City farm team. In this bleak moment, he would have done well to heed Hall of Fame pitcher Bob Feller's words: "Every day is a new opportunity. You can build on yesterday's success or put its failures behind and start over again. That's the way life is, with a new game every day. And that's the way baseball is."

Indeed, Taylor was way down—and on the verge of another comeback.

Meet the Mets' Most Unusual Player

Good old Bing Devine. Fired as Cardinals' general manager during the 1964 season, he caught on as Mets' G.M. in November, 1966. Remembering Taylor's contribution to the 1964 champions, Devine thought he could rebound if he changed teams. In early February of 1967, he called Taylor, then on the roster of

Houston's Triple-A team in Oklahoma City, and asked if he could still pitch. Taylor assured him he could. "Get me outta here!" he begged.

So the Mets bought his contract from Houston on February 10, and technically assigned him to their Triple-A team in Jacksonville. Technically, because they had higher hopes for him. The Mets invited Taylor to spring training, hoping he'd make the big club. "How many players get a better break than that?" Taylor said later.

He made an immediate impact. "The way he has been going, Taylor has to help us," New York manager Wes Westrum told Al Levine of the *St. Petersburg Times* in March. "I've said all along that we need a short man in our bullpen. That's where we lost a lot of ball games last season. Taylor definitely is a strong candidate."

Taylor made the club and the club stood by him when he relieved Don Cardwell on April 17, felt pain in his back and didn't pitch again for 36 days. Despite the layoff, Taylor was a workhorse. In 50 appearances, he went 4–6, with a 2.34 ERA and eight saves. At one point he allowed just one run in 16 games covering $24^2/_3$ innings. A website article under M.U.M. (Most Underrated Mets) claims Taylor had "the best stretch of any relief pitcher in the Mets' six-year history," with four wins, five saves and a 1.26 ERA in his last 38 appearances. And he could warm up faster than anyone else on the team.

If Taylor's pitching impressed his teammates, his personality staggered them. Taylor was a seasoned 29 now, with a reputation and a track record. He was free to be himself.

"My first impression about Ronnie was of an aloof character," outfielder Art Shamsky says. "He had wit and sarcasm and was able to needle people. Certainly the smartest guy in the room, he would sit on the floor reading with horn-rimmed glasses. He'd pick up on something, needle someone and go back to reading. He had a bizarre sense of humor. But we became friends, and I respected his intelligence."

Shamsky grew to appreciate Taylor's sangfroid. "He had a quietness about him that showed no panic. Ken Boswell and I nicknamed him Duke. He's just that: he's a duke. He's royalty."

"He was a kook," Joe Pignatano, the bullpen coach, says. "He was an oddball. He tried to stay by himself. Most of the time he'd sit there and say nothing. But he was a good guy. He had good stuff and was a battler; and Gil [Hodges, who soon became Mets manager] really liked him."

"He was a smart pitcher. He showed that by the way he located his pitches and handled the game. He put more pressure on himself than anyone else put on him. He came in to save a game for me one time and wound up losing it. That bothered him so much he didn't come to the room that night."

Rooming with Taylor was plainly beneficial to Koosman. "I sure do feel the pressure of the pennant race," he told Ira Berkow of Newspaper Enterprise Association. "Like this morning, I'm coming down the elevator of the hotel with my roomie, Ron Taylor, and I say, 'Ron, I wake up the day I'm going to pitch … It goes so slow. I sit around and worry about how I'm going to do.'

"Ron was with the Cardinals when they won pennants and he told me that it was just my way to get up for the game, that if I wasn't hung up like this I'd be overconfident. That would hurt."

They were some pair: Taylor the quiet, studious Canadian; Koosman the convivial Midwesterner. "Him and Koosie, that's a good quinella," their teammate Ed Kranepool puts it. "Koosie was so outgoing. Ronny was very introverted and stayed to himself. He didn't show much emotion and his face was somber. He was basically a loner; I was surprised he became a doctor. But [once you got him talking] he was bright and articulate, a great guy to be around and great conversation."

Taylor was gifted but he never played on it, a quality that his teammates respected. Taylor and his roomie had one quality in common. When Taylor spoke of Koosman's "discipline and intelligence" on the mound, he could have been talking about himself. The players were O.K. with Taylor's reading books like *Rickenbacker* in clubhouses, on planes, in hotel lobbies waiting for the team bus. He went through 100 or so books every year. Teammates also appreciated his quick wit. Taylor had a locker on one side of the clubhouse with Cal Koonce and Don Cardwell, who were from North Carolina, and a Virginian, J.C. Martin. Clubhouse custodian Nick Torman hung a sign over "Y'all's-Row." What was Taylor doing with three Southerners? "I'm from South Canada," he said in Stanley Cohen's *A Magic Summer: The '69 Mets*.

The 1967 Mets repeated in last place with a 61–101 record but the addition of future Hall-of-Famer Tom Seaver, a rookie who had a 16–13 record and 2.76 ERA, suggested better things were ahead. Nonetheless, Manager Wes Westrum, who had given Taylor a chance to pitch and resuscitated his career, resigned at the end of the season.

His replacement, Gil Hodges, had improved the Washington Senators in each of his five years with them. Hodges ordered curfews, jackets and ties on the road, and more drills on fundamentals. He took aside every Mets player, told him his responsibilities and insisted he be ready. If you were the right-handed pinch hitter, you felt good about it. You were THE right-handed pinch hitter. "Gil was a good guy and a smart guy and he died too young," Pignatano says. "He used to keep his door open because the players had to pass by his office. He'd whistle to get their attention, say, 'Come in,' and then he'd shut the door when they did. They'd talk about the games and how the player did and whether Gil thought it was right or wrong. He never disciplined any player. He never had to."

Though Taylor, like most pitchers, would have preferred to start and set the tempo for a game—he told the *Times*'s Robert Lipsyte he'd like to "take a shot at being a 20-game winner"—he readily acceded to Hodges' demand that he relieve. In fact, Taylor never once started a game for the Mets. Though his record slipped to 1–5, he led the 1968 team with 14 saves (all of which would count as saves today), gave up only one homer and allowed just 2.70 earned runs per nine innings. With Cal Koonce (11 saves, 2.42 ERA) also working short relief, the club had an effective one-two punch in the bullpen.

always in control. He was an athlete and a pitcher and an intellect and a good person. Those things don't happen all the time."

In the media capital of the world, Taylor was nothing if not a witty interview subject. "Relief pitchers lead the lonely life," Vic Ziegel wrote in the *New York Post*. "Their careers are precarious, they are used at nervous moments in a game, one wrong pitch and they have failed, one right pitch and the starting pitcher or the team's home-run hitter is a hero.

"Recently, Ron Taylor saved a game and said, 'When the game's at stake … that's when it's fun to pitch.'

"Taylor came into a tie game in the Mets' very next contest [actually two games later], walked the first two batters he faced, was pulled, and became the losing pitcher. 'I just want you to know,' he told a reporter later, 'that it's still fun.'"

On another occasion, Taylor said, "Doubleheader tomorrow, barring nuclear holocaust."

New York was Fun City for Taylor, and he made it a better place for others. An undated letter to a New York paper from one Barry Farber of Bayside, New York, said in part:

"At a banquet this winter at our temple, Ron Taylor of the Mets was not only a fine speaker and guest but he did something that we might term a mitzvah (good deed). After his appearance at our temple, he readily agreed to visit a young man in our community who, though he has muscular dystrophy, is a great sports enthusiast.

"Ron spent some time in this young man's house and on leaving promised to write. Though a good many promises are made merely for "courtesy" sake, Ron not only wrote and sent pictures but asked if there was anything further he could do. His reward, I hope, is knowing of the great joy he brought to this young man."

The Mets moved up a notch to ninth with a 73–89 record in 1968 and Koosman, who would become one of baseball's best left-handers, had a 19-win rookie season. But no one expected the Mets, a 100-to-1 to win the pennant in 1969, to come home.

Actually, there was some question whether the 1969 season would start at all. Pitchers and catchers usually report to spring training camps by Feb. 15 but many held out in February 1969. Everyday players, due to report March 1, supported them and threatened their own boycott. Ballplayers were upset that the owners hadn't made promised contributions from broadcast revenues to the pension fund. In St. Petersburg, Tom Seaver and several other Mets, including Taylor, organized informal workouts at a small park. Mostly they conducted hour-long workouts while kidding with the press.

In 1969, the average salary was $24,909, with Willie Mays the best-paid player at $135,000. As David Halberstam wrote in *October 1964*, "No other profession in the country left talented men with so little control over their own destiny and deprived them of their true market value."

The immortal Marvin Miller had been elected executive director of the Major League Baseball Players' Association in 1966, and he had made a start in righting the imbalance. In 1968, he negotiated baseball's first collective bargaining agreement (CBA), a two-year deal winning a 43 percent increase in the minimum salary from $7,000 to $10,000 and larger expense allowances, while formalizing the structure of player-owner relations and establishing arbitration of grievances before the commissioner. But it was still a nascent union needing courage and leadership. Respected men like Seaver and Taylor provided it.

Taylor was working out on a high-school diamond in St. Petersburg, Florida with, as he recalls, fellow pitchers Al Jackson, Jerry Koosman and Seaver, plus catcher Jerry Grote and first baseman-outfielder Ed Kranepool. But when it came time to step up and address the issues seriously, Taylor was front and center.

"It's not a question of pension; it's a question of principle,"

said, 'Are you guys getting in shape?' We said we were. 'Good. Because you four'—referring to Koosman, Seaver, Jackson and me—'are going to throw as soon as this is over.' Sure enough, he had us pitching an inning apiece when the games started."

The clubs were considering the use of replacement players. However, new commissioner Bowie Kuhn, working behind the scenes to avoid beginning his tenure with a damaging labor problem, settled the dispute with a three-year, $5.4-million-per-year deal. The time of eligibility for a pension was reduced from five to four years of service, with early retirement set at 45. Widow, maternity and disability benefits were increased. Meanwhile, Taylor signed a one-year contract for $23,000. But the biggest payday for him was the pension he would retire on. Cashing his $38,295.50 annual check helped him start a medical practice.

To be sure, the 1969 club was likely to improve. Another good rookie pitcher, Gary Gentry, joined the club. Center fielder Tommie Agee was on target after a rough 1968. On June 15, 1969, the Mets picked up Donn Clendenon, a tough, unsparing first baseman and a right-handed power bat, from Montreal. In *The New York Mets*, Jack Lang called it "the deal of the decade."

"When Clendenon joined us, we started to win more and began to jell," outfielder Ron Swoboda told teammate Art Shamsky, who wrote a book about the 1969 New York baseball, basketball and football champions called *The Magnificent Seasons.* "Clende-non had a way about him. He had been on a good team. He could annoy the crap out of you, but he had this way where you could get back at him. Suddenly, we were a real good team."

Equally uncompromising, Seaver told teammates that a .500 season would be nothing to crow about. "There was an aura of defeat," he told Bill Leggett of *Sports Illustrated*, "and I refused to accept it. Maybe some of the others started to feel how I felt because I noticed that the team seemed to play better behind me than it did for any other pitcher." Seaver won 25 games and the Cy Young Award.

It was as if the team had been put together by a Broadway producer. Shamsky was the designated Jewish sage who would or-ganize team reunions after everyone retired. Third baseman Ed (The Glider) Charles, was a smooth fielder, poet and calming in-fluence: an African-American *griot.* Jerry Grote, who insisted the Mets could win the "whole shootin' match," was the Texan catch-er, annoying but inspiring his teammates and almost unmatched on defensive skills. "If I was on the same team with him, I'd have to play third base," Hall of Fame catcher Johnny Bench said. Clendenon had a couple of semesters of law school. Cal Koonce collected art. Jack DeLauro did a hilarious imitation of the televi-sion impresario Ed Sullivan. Hodges, who privately hoped for 85 wins, convinced the players at four positions that platooning was in their best interest. In an especially dramatic scene on July 30, he walked out to left field to remove Cleon Jones, who he didn't think was hustling. That was considered a defining moment for the team.

Where did Taylor fit in? "We had a young pitching staff with guys like Tom Seaver, Jerry Koosman and Gary Gentry; and [Cal] Koonce, [Don] Cardwell and Taylor were a stabilizing force," Cleon Jones says. "Taylor always wanted the ball, no matter what the score was."

When the Mets were winning 11 straight and advancing from losers to potential contenders between May 28 and June 10, he had four saves and two wins. Maybe the highlight was the game of May 30, in which he struck out future Hall of Famers Willie

Mays and Willie McCovey, while preserving Seaver's 1–0 shutout over the Giants. Or maybe the highlight was the two scoreless innings he pitched to beat the Dodgers 1–0 on June 4. "The Mets became a real team last night," Maury Allen wrote in the Post, "a serious team, an exciting team for positive things instead of nasty negatives." When Taylor inadvertently banged his elbow on a locker days later, Casey Stengel said, "The ...

... Ferguson Jenkins 4–3, on Kranepool's dying-quail blooper past shortstop. Some felt that game, rather than the June 4 one, was the day the Mets coalesced as a team. In any case, Seaver threw a gem the next day; and Taylor had three saves in four days, one against the Expos on July 13, two in Chicago on July 15 and 16.

Everything they did was magnified by the New York-area media. Dick Schaap and Paul D. Zimmerman edited a contrived, you-are-there book called *The Year the Mets Lost Last Place*. Using sportswriters to do their research and breathless present tense, they traced "nine crucial days" in July that supposedly turned the Mets into contenders. At least the saves on July 15 and 16 in Chicago allowed Taylor some moments of microscoped greatness and personality. He entered the July 15 game with a one-run lead and two outs in the eighth after Billy Williams and Ron Santo had homered. Under 3:15 p.m.:

> A quiet college man, with a degree in electrical engineering and collections of stamps, jazz records and tropical fish, Taylor survives in the big leagues on intelligence, a good sinker and a sense of humor. "What do I have to work with?" he says. "Well, a little sinker, a slider that backs up some days and a change or two … you know, mediocre stuff."
>
> Taylor reaches the mound, and Hodges flips him the ball. "You got a run," says the manager, "and nobody on."

Taylor gets Ernie Banks to pop up for the final out of the eighth inning.

Under 3:50 p.m.:

The Cubs come up in the bottom of the ninth, for one more shot at Ron Taylor and his mediocre stuff.

On a two-and-two count to Willie Smith, a power hitter, Taylor throws his slider, the pitch that sometimes backs up. Smith swings and strikes out.

[The account neglects to mention that Taylor struck out Randy Hundley for the second out.]

Jimmy Qualls, the man who spoiled Tom Seaver's perfect game, comes to bat. Qualls has two for three already today; he is batting .385 against the Mets. On Taylor's second pitch, Qualls hits a ground ball to Ed Kranepool at first base. Taylor rushes toward first, Kranepool flips him the ball, Taylor steps on the bag and the game is over. The Mets win, 5–4. Even the Bleacher Bums are still.

After saving a 9–5 game for Seaver the following day, Taylor shows up again. Under 5:09 p.m.:

In the Met clubhouse, Ron Taylor, the relief pitcher, turns to a reporter. "Are the nine crucial days over yet?" he asks, mocking the phrase used to describe the games with the Cubs and Montreal Expos.

"Not till midnight," says the reporter.

"Then all that's left," replies Taylor, "is the crucial plane ride to Montreal."

The Mets were still in second place, but the book ended there. To be fair, they were playing exquisite ball. "Good young pitching," Taylor told *The New York Times*'s Joseph Durso. "The Mets are always in the game with Seaver and Koosman." And Gentry (13–12, 3.43 ERA). Good older pitching, too.

On July 20, the Mets huddled in the Montreal airport to watch men walk on the moon and concluded, "That was an impossible dream. We can do the same." On August 1, in the game Taylor referenced in his address at the Empire Club, Taylor reluctantly gave Henry Aaron an intentional pass to put runners on first and second with two outs and a one-run lead over the Braves, then retired Orlando Cepeda on a grounder to second, ending the game.

Still trailing Chicago by 9½ games on August 13, the Mets swept a doubleheader in which Taylor saved a 1–0 game for Seaver on August 16 and launched into a streak in which they won 38 of their last 49 games. When the Mets finally took first place on September 10, with shreds of newspaper flying from the stands and the scoreboard rejoiced "We're Number one!" Taylor got the win that put them there in a 13-inning 4–3 game against

Army reserve duty that took us away on some weekends and four two weeks in the summer. Platooning was another big reason we were fresh. You add up the RBIs at each position where Gil platooned—Swoboda and Shamsky in right (99), Clendenon and Kranepool at first (86), Al Weis and me at second (55), Ed Charles and Wayne Garrett at third (57)—and you see what you've got. All 25 guys contributed—it wasn't just the Tom [Seaver] and Jerry [Koosman] show. That endeared us to the fans. And we had coaches from winning traditions—Rube Walker (pitching), Yogi Berra (first base), Eddie Yost (third base) and Joe Pignatano (bullpen)—who kept us pointed in the right direction." (That was generous. The great bulk of Yost's career had been with the lowly Washington Senators.)

"This was more fun than '64," said Taylor, who won four, saved four and recorded a 1.80 ERA over the last two months. "This time we won it going away. In '64, we went down to the last game of the season."

Comparing the two clubs, he said, "I like this one. It's a younger team with a great pitching staff."

Taylor had one concern that he explained to the *Toronto Star*'s Milt Dunnell. "I guess you read about our pennant party? All the champagne, I mean. I did a lot of extra running to make up for that."

Tug McGraw (9–3, 12 saves, 2.24 ERA) had almost an identical season as Taylor (9–4, 13 saves, 2.70 ERA). They couldn't have been more different: Taylor, the serious sinker-slider guy; McGraw, who threw and was a screwball. "I wish I could have been more like Tug McGraw," Taylor told Bruce Markusen, author of *Tales From the Mets Dugout*. "I'm kind of a quiet and laid-back person. Tug was always up front and entertaining people."

Hodges called on the veteran first when the Mets took on the Atlanta Braves in the National League Championship Series. The Mets had won eight of 12 games with the Braves but were considered underdogs. In Game One, Seaver allowed five runs in seven shaky innings before the Mets erupted for five of their own off Phil Niekro, .209-hitting J.C. Martin contributing a two-run single in the eighth and presenting Taylor with a 9–5 lead.

"Old Ron Taylor came to Seaver's rescue and was as reliable as a mother's smile," Canadian journalist Rex Edmonston wrote.

"I applaud Gil Hodges for going to his bullpen, just when he did, and asking Mr. Taylor to finish the job," said Reds' Manager Dave Bristol.

Taylor threw two shutout innings, allowing only one walk, to hold the 9–5 lead. This might be a good time to spell out the save discrepancy. Pre-1969, a reliever who went to work with any kind of lead and finished the game with the lead intact qualified for a save. Today's save requirements are much more restrictive:

A pitcher must finish a game won by his team;

He can't be the winning pitcher;

He must pitch at least one-third of an inning; and

He satisfies one of the following conditions:

He enters with a maximum three-run lead and pitches for at least one inning;

He enters with the potential tying run on base, at bat or on deck; or

He pitches for at least three innings.

Because he preserved a four-run lead and only pitched two innings, Taylor's splendid effort didn't qualify for a save in 1969. So what? It was just what the team needed. "I gave up five runs and still won the game!" Seaver yelled in the clubhouse. "God truly is a Met!"

Taylor had a very different relief assignment in Game Two. Another expected pitcher's duel blew up when the Mets and Jerry Koosman took a 9–1 lead over Ron Reed. Koosman came apart in the fifth inning. With two out, he yielded a single to Felix Milan,

Mets batted, astounding broadcaster Tony Kubek. Then Taylor pitched a scoreless sixth, striking out two; and McGraw held off the Braves with a three-inning stint. Final score: Mets 11, Braves 6, with Taylor getting the win and McGraw the save.

Yet another pitching duel evaporated when the Mets' Gentry lasted only two innings in Game Three. And yet another sterling relief job appeared like a genie from a bottle: Nolan Ryan went seven innings to give the Mets a series sweep 7–4. With a win and a save that wasn't, Taylor admitted, "To have affected two of the three games was great." Casey Stengel, who had managed the Mets in their first 3½ dour seasons, said, "The team has come along slow, but fast." Umpire Ed Sodom said, "I had them [the Mets] a lot of times this year, but this was the greatest thrill. They're appropriately named the Amazing Mets. They've come from the depths of despair to the celestial. I studied literature and made that up myself."

At a reception thrown by New York Governor Nelson Rockefeller and his wife Happy, Taylor told Maury Allen, "You know, my in-laws don't want me to play baseball. They wonder what I'm doing when I could be a big, famous engineer. But I'm doing what makes me happy. I have a Phi Beta Kappa in engineering and I'd rather be here, be a Met, be with this team."

The Orioles were 8-to-5 bets to beat the Mets in the 1969 World Series. And Baltimore newspapers were crowning their beloved Birds after Mike Cuellar beat Seaver 4–1 in the Baltimore opener. Don Cardwell pitched one scoreless, hitless inning in relief; and Taylor pitched the last two innings, allowing no runs, no hits and one walk while fanning three. Almost unnoticed, he struck out Frank Robinson and Brooks Robinson, while picking Paul Blair off of first. The game ended when Art Shamsky grounded out with two runners on and two out in the ninth. On a team noted for its starting pitchers, the relievers once again kept them in the game. As the Mets left the field, Ed Charles told Oriole coach George Bamberger, "That's the last game you guys are going to win." Bamberger said, "You've got to be kidding." The Orioles were jumping and having fun. The Series was over, at least as far as Baltimore sportswriters were concerned.

That feeling wasn't shared in the Mets clubhouse. Clendenon told Seaver, "We're going to beat these guys. They didn't get the real you, and they get Koosman tomorrow."

"One game doesn't make a series, I wasn't worried at all," Taylor later told Shamsky. "I pitched in the 1964 World Series for the Cardinals and we were underdogs to the Yankees. The series went seven games and we won. You just can't get discouraged after one game. With the Mets we had a team that came back all the time during the season. And with Jerry Koosman pitching the next day, we knew we would have a chance."

Indeed, in Game Two Koosman pitched six no-hit innings against Dave McNally and took a 2–1 lead into last of the ninth on a Clendenon homer and a run-scoring single by .215-hitting Al Weis. With two out, Koosman walked Frank Robinson and Boog Powell. Hodges took the ball from Koosman, who walked off the field to a standing ovation from the Baltimore fans, no sportswriters, they. Hodges called on Taylor, the team's only World Series veteran, and for what it's worth, the only Met on the postseason roster born outside the U.S. Hodges told him, "You've got to get one man out."

Brooks Robinson, who had driven in Paul Blair in the seventh, came to the plate. The runners would be going on contact, and anything through the infield would score the tying run. "Losing the first two games to the 109-win Orioles would almost certainly spell doom for the Mets in the World Series," the redoubtable M.U.M. wrote.

It was another existential moment in another World Series, one fraught with tension. Except Taylor didn't see it that way. As

... have overpowering stuff, so I've got to get ahead of the guy. I was pretty damn worried."

Taylor got a called strike. With the count 3–2 and two out, the runners were moving when bat met ball. On a good sinker, Brooks grounded to third baseman Charles, who thought about running to the bag for a force but wouldn't have won the race there against Merv Rettenmund, who was running for Frank Robinson. Somewhat tentatively, Charles threw to first. The throw arrived short and low, but Donn Clendenon dug it out of the dirt well ahead of the slow and chugging Robinson, who hit into several triple plays during his Hall of Fame career. Game over. If the ball had escaped Clendenon, at the very least Rettenmund would have scored to tie the score and Powell would have stood on third. Don't even think of it.

"Facing Robinson with two out and two on was the toughest one-on-one test of my career," Taylor said after the game.

"I had to keep the ball down and hopefully get a ground ball," he continued. "It was kind of simple. I was just missing off the plate. Brooks was an icon. I was just a player. But I never felt overwhelmed. It was all in terms of focus."

"Once more! Look up, Ron!" Photographers chimed in the Mets clubhouse.

"I'm not much of a smiler," Taylor said. Down to his gray, sweat-stained underwear, Taylor put a foot up on a three-legged

stool and stripped the tab off a can of beer. "I'm really a strug-
gler," he said. "I've probably got more native ability as an engineer than a ballplayer.

"But I like baseball." He turned more serious. It had been a
bad year by some standards—Chappaquiddick, disclosure of the
1968 Mi Lai massacre, among other downers—and an especially
troubling year in New York City.

Things could have been worse, but "Look what the Mets have
done for New York this year," Taylor said. "The crime rate is
down and the riots have been fewer. We're responsible for part of
that. The whole town's hooked on the Mets.

"It's only a game, I know. But it's better than what's happening in Vietnam or the Middle East. It's a game, but it brings people together." A particular beneficiary was Mayor John Lindsay.
Denied the Republican nomination for re-election, shunted to the
Liberal Party's name on the ballot, he was re-elected in part, political observers swear, because of his identification with the Mets.

Though Taylor wasn't needed in the remainder of the postseason, Brooks Robinson felt the Series hinged on the second game.
Shamsky believed that if the Mets lost Game Two, they might
have been swept. In *The Magnificent Seasons*, Shamsky writes,
"Ron Taylor never got the recognition that he deserved for his
heroics with our club."

There was plenty of excitement to come. Agee led off Game
Three with a homer and made two spectacular catches, probably
saving five runs—all Gentry and Ryan needed to shut out the Orioles, 5–0. With the Mets and Seaver leading the Orioles and Cuellar in Game Four, 1–0, in the ninth inning, Baltimore put runners
on first and third and Brooks Robinson hit a sinking liner to right-
center that appeared certain to tie the game and might go through
to score two runners. Except that Ron Swoboda, no Roberto Clemente in right, made a great diving catch to hold the Orioles to
one run on the sacrifice fly. "The bottom line is, some guys had
a career—I had a catch," Swoboda told Shamsky. The Mets won
in the 10th when J.C. Martin laid down a bunt with runners on
first and second, and the throw to first caromed off his shoulder
and bounced toward short right field, scoring Rod Gaspar. Seaver,

pitching with a strained left-calf muscle, went the distance.

The finale, Game Five, was kismet, bedlam and four-leaf clo-ver rolled into one. The Mets were trailing, 3–0 when Cleon Jones led off the bottom of the sixth. McNally threw inside to him and the ball squirted into the Met dugout. Home plate umpire Lou DiMuro made no call but Hodges emerged from the dugout hold-

dropped Powell's throw. Now it was 5–3. With Powell on first in the ninth, Davey Johnson hit a deep drive to left, everyone in Shea Stadium gagging. The ball came down in Cleon Jones's glove as he dropped to one knee, and a classic of a Fall Classic was over. The Series MVP could have been Koosman, Weis, Agee, Swoboda, Clendenon (the winner) or a leprechaun.

The last word belonged to Casey Stengel, the Old Perfesser, the Mets' first manager. "This club doesn't make many mistakes now, you can see they believe in each other, and the coaches all live in New York and you can get them on the phone," Stengel said. "So I'm very proud of these fellas, which did such a splendid job; and if they keep improving like this, they can keep going to Christmas. The Mets are amazing."

The Mets rode down the Canyon of Heroes in a ticker-tape parade, with fans ripping buttons off their blazers and molding off the cars. "I couldn't stop thinking that this was the path that Ma-cArthur, Eisenhower and Kennedy had ridden," Taylor told Mau-ry Allen for his book *After the Miracle: The Amazing Mets—Two Decades Later.* "I never felt so euphoric."

It had been a spectacular season for any team in any city. The fact that it occurred in New York magnified the accomplishment. The Mets made the covers of *Time* and *Life* and appeared on the "Ed Sullivan Show" to sing "You Gotta Have Heart." Seven Mets sang "The Impossible Dream" in Las Vegas. Ken Boswell, Rod Gaspar and Wayne Garrett appeared on "The Dating Game." Mark Rudd, student revolutionary, told the *Post*'s Larry Merchant that sports are the opiate of the masses. "The Mets, however, are symbolic to us of what the movement can accomplish. If a handful of Mets can go to the top, so too can a handful of revolutionaries." Pete Hamill of the *Post* wrote about his father's attendance at the last game of Series: "He was there because the Mets are the last romantics, men who believed in themselves more than anyone else did, men who believed in possibilities." Future New York Governor Mario Cuomo, quoted in Shamsky's book, said, "The Mets were a bunch of really good players who were not perceived as great. They weren't a dynasty by any means. They were underdogs who were winning. And when they won, all those immigrants and sons and daughters of immigrants, and the poor people following the team won, because you were the underdog."

Beau comme le jour. In the champagne celebration, a television interviewer asked Taylor how he was going to celebrate. 'I'm going to John Patrick's Pub," he said, referring to a bar the middleweight boxing champion, Taylor's friend Joey Archer, owned across the street from where Don Cardwell and Taylor lived at 333 E. 80th St. at the corner of First Avenue.

"When we got there, they were lined up around the block," Taylor says. "It was as if World War II had just ended." After a drink at the bar, he and Cardwell changed clothes and went to Diamond Club at Shea Stadium for a party.

Taylor visited the Toronto mayor's office, where he was given golf cuff links. He gave speeches at $150 to $300 a shot. Combined with his $23,000 salary and $18,300 Series share, that made for a profitable year. The Mets increased his salary to $28,000, the most he would ever make as a ballplayer.

Taylor returned to New York before spring training and touched one player in a special place. "I received a letter from the Montreal Expos to report to Homestead, Florida spring of '70," Owen Kelly wrote on Ultimate Mets Database. "During the winter months I needed a place to throw, so a buddy of mine wrote to the director of the YMCA in Flushing, Queens, and got me in.

What I did not know was that Ron Taylor and Duffy Dyer were also working out at the YMCA. To make a long story short, both were great, but Ron was special. I remember our last days of talks and I remember this [as] if it was yesterday. He told me he wanted to play a few more years, get his pension, then go to Medical School, and he already had an engineering degree. When he said

faced, Taylor got the first Opening Day win in Mets history when his teammates rallied for two ninth-inning runs to beat the Pirates 5–3. The team came down to earth soon enough and finished third at 83–79. Taylor had his usual 13 saves, but 11 of them were in the first half-season. There just weren't that many save opportunities when the team closed at 27–33 over their last 60 games, and Taylor blew two of his last four save chances while his ERA climbed to 3.93.

Today, 33 is middle-aged but still breathing in baseball. In 1971, determined to go with a "youth" movement, the Mets used 25-year-old Danny Frisella and 26-year-old Tug McGraw for short relief. Relegated to middle relief and mop-up, Taylor had just two saves. Fortunately, he also had an experience that made the year worthwhile. Tom Seaver introduced him to George H. W. Bush, the U.N. ambassador, who later was vice president and president; and they became friends. Bush had been captain of the Yale varsity and knew a lot about baseball. "We talked about strategy," Taylor said. "Just a very pleasant man. I respected him, and we had rapport." They became correspondents, and Bush later sent Taylor his congratulations for being accepted at medical school.

Taylor was purchased by Montreal in the off-season. The Expos released him before he'd pitched an inning, and San Diego signed him. His fastball gone, Taylor retired after four dispiriting games with the Padres. The decision was a slam dunk. Taylor knew he was finished playing baseball. As former infielder Roy Smalley memorably put it, "When you've been through what I've been through, you have to come to grips with your own culpability."

At San Diego General Manager Buzzie Bavasi's request, Taylor stuck around the rest of the season to pitch batting practice and do some promotions. It was a nice gesture by Bavasi and an even nicer acceptance by Taylor, who could have taken his severance check and gone home.

Did anyone take notice of what Taylor accomplished in his five seasons with the Mets? The club's first closer used exclusively as a reliever, he left with 50 saves, a team record at the time, and led the Mets in the category every year from 1967 through 1970. His 269 appearances were another team record then. His WHIP (walks plus hits per nine innings) of 1.14 is the lowest of any Mets reliever who pitched as many as his 361 innings, as is his average of 0.598 homers per nine innings. He was at his absolute best in the postseason. "At a time when no one expected the Mets to win," M.U.M. concludes, "Ron Taylor was truly just what the doctor ordered." The verdict: "a most salutary purchase," in the words of baseball author Donald Honig.

There's no statistic less relevant than won-lost record for a reliever, especially if he's a closer. He gets losses for blowing leads, and wins for blowing leads and sticking around while his teammates get them back. Hall of Famer Bruce Sutter, who never once started, had a 68–71 mark. Taylor, who started 17 times in 491 appearances, went 45–43 (3–9 as a starter, 42–34 as a reliever), with 72 saves, a 3.93 ERA, a 1.25 WHIP and a 2.22 strikeout-to-walk ratio. He made three errors in 11 seasons. But few if any players threw seven no-hit innings in four World-Series outings, or had a 0.00 ERA, three saves and a win over $10^{1}/_{3}$ postseason innings covering six games.

Now, seven innings is a small sample. We'll never know how Taylor would have stacked up over a longer haul against, say, the incomparable Mariano Rivera. In 24 Series appearances, Rivera had 19 saves and an 0.99 ERA. But nowhere in the $36^{1}/_{3}$ innings he pitched was there a run of seven consecutive hitless ones. The best he did was $6\frac{1}{3}$ in 2000–01. Rivera did go nine hitless innings in the 1998 postseason, but not the Series.

Taylor never spent much time pondering his stats. He was already looking ahead.

On To Medical School

sight of doctors attending to the wounded. Suddenly, he realized: medicine was an opportunity for him to help people more than engineering or baseball ever did.

In 1968 he toured Okinawa and Guam with the Tigers' Denny McLain and the Chicago White Sox' Montrealer Pete Ward. The following year saw Taylor in Vietnam, where he learned that soldiers had fired off their guns to celebrate the Mets' championship. In 1970 he visited Guam and the other stops in the Pacific theater.

"I was happy and fulfilled I was able to be there and be supportive under those conditions," Taylor said.

Taylor made sure to take down the addresses and phone numbers of the soldiers' parents, write to them and call them. "It was late 1969 or early 1970," Dennis M. Lyons reported on Ultimate Mets Database, "when I met Ron Taylor and several other baseball players in Nam. They were on a USO tour that winter, visiting U.S. personnel. I was with a few other men at a table in a club on a base that had a hospital that the tour just visited. Ron sat with us, bought us a beer, and talked to us. He was interested in how we built highways through the rice paddies. I was impressed with the fact that he was so real. You know what I mean, he could have just talked about himself, the series, but he wanted to know about us and what we did.

"I was lucky enough to meet with another USO tour group that included the Commissioner of baseball and several other famous players. Bigger names than Ron Taylor. But it was Ron that impressed me the most that winter in Nam, again because of the way he treated us that day.

"Ron never got a chance to finish his beer that day. He said that happened a lot, they kept him moving. A truly amazing Met. Thanks for the beer Ron. I owe you one."

After the last visit, in 1970, to Japan, Okinawa, Guam and the Philippines with Hall of Fame pitcher Waite Hoyt, the Pirates' Richie Hebner, the Royals' Ed Kirkpatrick, and retired umpire Jocko Conlin, Taylor reported that fewer beds were filled and maybe the war was winding down.

The soldiers flown in from Vietnam didn't want to talk about the war, but what had happened to the Mets. "I took the rap before anybody could put it on me," Taylor told Allen of the *New York Post*. "I told them a lot of us, including myself, didn't have as good years as we had the year before."

Turning more serious, he added, "A lot of the kids were just waiting to go home from there. It's an awfully long time when you just lie in bed and wait. The only thing we could do was show them we were interested in them. They really seem to appreciate that. They were thankful we came. That made the trip worthwhile."

Old friend Bill Forder, a urological surgeon, urged him to go to medical school once he quit pitching. He already had a bedside manner. On December 23, 1970, Taylor visited Booth Memorial Medical Center in New York's Flushing, Queens. He handed out Mets' yearbooks, autographs and good cheer to a ward full of children. Then, to his delight, he met an oldster as quick with a word as he was. Their conversation was captured by Phil Pepe of the *New York Daily News*.

"Hi, I'm Ron Taylor of the Mets. They call me 'Throw it and duck Taylor.'"

"It's maybe on account of you that I'm in here with the heart attack," the patient, a cabdriver from Jackson Heights named Irving Liner, said. "What happened? I want to know what happened?"

"You think I had a bad year, huh?" Taylor said.

"At the beginning, you were going like a house on fire," Liner said, "but at the end, oh, boy. I think it was a letdown on the whole team. Who was there to beat? Pittsburgh was a mishmash."

"You really lay it on the line, don't you, Irving?"

"So, I listen to the game, and you come in and bang, there was a home run. So what am I going to say?"

"Now you're trying to smooth it over, Irving." Taylor was pretending to be offended, but really enjoying himself, Pepe wrote.

"I think," Liner said after a few more minutes, "that this is the best thing that happened to me in months. I think you're doing a great thing coming here."

Two years later Taylor did another great thing. When the Montreal Expos demoted him to Triple-A before he'd played in one regular-season game, he asked for his release and got it. Taylor called up his old Cardinal teammate Roger Craig, who was pitching coach for the San Diego Padres; and the club decided to take a chance on him.

It was a young team, and Taylor's arm was quitting on him. He was released after four appearances. Peter Bavasi, running the Padres' farm system then, now retired and fly-fishing in the Pacific Ocean, remembers approaching Taylor at his locker to discuss a severance payout. "He didn't want it!" Bavasi said. "I said, 'We can't do that. But can we help you find your next career path?' He said, 'No, I'm going to become a doctor.'"

But first Taylor finished the season pitching batting practice and traveling with the team. "A lot of players have trouble adjusting to life after baseball," he said. "I'm grateful to the Padres for letting me stay with the club [and get baseball out of his system]. It was a key transition point."

When the Padres were in Montreal, Taylor took a side trip and had his fateful interview at the University of Toronto Medical School. "He called me up one day and said, 'Don, I'm washed up,'" Don Patrick, his Houston surgeon friend, says.

"'What now?' I asked him.

"'I'm thinking about medical school.'

"'Ron, they don't have a tendency to accept people that age because it's a long grind. I had a five-year residency, plus two more in the army. You need to be a lawyer. You've got a good way about you, because people trust you.'

"'That's what medicine is like.'

"'Three years and you can catch on with a firm.'

"He still wanted to be a doctor."

Fulfilling a final pledge to his last major-league team, the San Diego Padres, Taylor also spent the summer of 1973 managing the Lethbridge Lakers of the semipro Alberta Major League, a San Diego affiliate, and took them to the national finals in New Brunswick.

Then it was on to medical school at the University of Toronto. These days plenty of people in their mid-30s enter medical school. In 1973, Taylor's matriculation staggered classmates and professors alike.

Taylor's first year of medical school consisted of more courses that were pure memory. It was especially difficult because as an engineering major years earlier he had to understand the laws of physics rather than memorize information. "He came in with a bunch of students for a seminar," Gross says. "I thought he was from the cleaning staff. He had to work harder than the other students because of his age, but I don't think he had any problems."

Not that he didn't look and act a trifle weird to his fellow students. He treated the cleaning staff with the same respect as his professors. He sat in the back of the room in a dirty old warm-up jacket. "Ron was in my basic neurology class," said Mike Bertram, his old professor. "He was a very mature, excellent student; and he worked his butt off. I was amazed how he could concentrate after a career involving so much revelry, but he was serious. It was a tremendous readjustment for him. He reminded me of servicemen's classes we had after World War II. It was a pleasure to lecture to them, and we would double the classes to accommodate them. They knew what they wanted and were willing to work very hard for it. Ron was the same. He knew that pro baseball wasn't a lifetime job."

Humor creeps into any discussion of Taylor. "In a practical

get up at 6, go over and have a cup of coffee with him. 'How are you doing?' he'd ask me. I said, 'Fine.' He went on, 'I'll never support you unless you deserve it.' I thought that was great. And he became a patient of mine."

Taylor moved smoothly to internship, where the problem-solving skills he learned at engineering school came in handy. "I think that's when Allan Gross and I became friends," Taylor said. "He was one of the high-profile specialists who were very gracious in the care of my patients."

One Day In the Life of Ron Taylor

In the last full calendar year of his medical career—he retired on June 30, 2014—Taylor arrived at his Toronto medical office at 7:00 a.m. one Tuesday in May, 2013. The office occupied the ground floor of a three-story brick building in a lively commercial section of town. As a concession to advancing age, Taylor no longer reported at 6 a.m. and instead worked four 10-hour days a week instead of five. He had a busy practice. But he also, as you'd discover from reading his 20-page C.V., found time to work as a staff physician and director of the S. C. Cooper Sports Medicine Clinic at the celebrated Mt. Sinai Hospital downtown; a lecturer at the University of Toronto medical School; a team doctor emeritus for the Toronto Blue Jays and a member of the Advisory Board for the Canadian Baseball Hall of Fame and Museum.

Well-organized as ever, Taylor sat behind cups of paper clips, pencils and pens; a Scotch Tape dispenser; and a stapler. A poster adorned the wall showing a *Toronto Star Weekly* write-up of Babe Ruth from the 1914 game—he was playing for Providence at Toronto—in which he hit his first professional homer and threw a one-hit shutout. Books like *Diseases of the Skin, Atlas of Human Anatomy* and *The Ultimate Back Book* lined the shelves. Quotes and definitions from a desk calendar filled Taylor's notebooks. Hardly the humorous flimflam you see on executives' calendars, they provide lessons and knowledge: "Faced with what is right, to leave it undone shows a lack of courage"—Confucius. "A man who wastes one hour of time has not discovered the value of life"—Charles Darwin.

Taylor stole a glance at the calendar between patients. "It's interesting when you turn a page and see something like that," he said.

Dressed in sneakers and sweatpants, as well as the green undershirt and white coat that many doctors wear, he looked better than he felt. By eating only two meals a day and cutting back on fatty foods, he'd lost 30 pounds and was back to his big-league fighting trim of 190 pounds (he'd lost an inch or so off his 6'2"). But he also suffered from polymyalgia rheumatica (PMR), an autoimmune disease that stimulates arthritis and causes aching and stiffness in the upper arms, neck, lower back and thighs. "All movement is tough," he said. "It affects sleep, and you're waking up with pain. When you wake up several times a night, it makes you irritable."

Taylor was in his fourth year of PMR, which typically lasts five years, though he never missed a day's work except when he had surgery. But he will never again walk as he used to. In 2012, his good friend Allan Gross, a surgeon, removed parts of three toes from Taylor's left foot. "They were lots of little fractures from landing on my left foot when I was pitching," Taylor explained. He also admitted his memory wasn't what it used to be.

One might wonder why he was still working at 75.

"I love what I'm doing," Taylor said. Other than a fondness

for baseball, military literature and military films, he had precious few hobbies.

Taylor had a family practice for patients 18 and older. "He spends time with his people," said a longtime patient, Toby Condliffe. "He speaks with you as well as treats you. You don't feel you're on an assembly line being rushed through."

she asked Taylor.

"Yeah, I know great ones, but you're beautiful," he said. "I can't understand why you need surgery."

She wanted to have her nose slightly flattened. "You don't need it, but I can recommend one, the one who did my nose," Taylor said.

"Do you know anyone else?" she asked.

"One thing I really treasure is the fun I've had with patients," Taylor said. He once had a consultation with Tim Crabtree of the Blue Jays, who had just earned his first save. "You have no idea how good it feels," Crabtree said.

"No, I couldn't imagine that," Taylor replied deadpan.

Taylor used a cell phone only on the road and got email from his wife Rona's computer. "He's very conservative: the way he dresses, the way he thinks," says Gross, the chief of surgery emeritus at Mount Sinai. "If he lived in the U.S., he'd be an old-style Republican. One of his strengths in medicine is that he knows when to punt: when a case should be referred to a specialist. He surrounded himself with specialists, with a cadre for every specialty. That's a real strength for him: he knows how to take care of his patients."

Most of his patients on this particular day came for routine treatment: physicals, shots, prescriptions, diagnoses. All of his work was satisfying. Occasionally, as when he conducted a routine examination of a 55-year-old businessman, discovered cancer of the prostate and got him a quick prostatectomy, he gets that warm glow comparable to what he accomplished in the World Series.

Taylor had a wedding ring and four World-Series rings—one with the Mets, one with the Cardinals and two for his work with the championship Blue Jays in 1992 and 1993—but he wore only the iron ring honoring his engineering degree. (He still has dinner with old engineering classmates every few months.) When word of his past glory leaked out to patients, Taylor finally mounted in the lobby a photo of himself pitching in the World Series for the Mets, his glove-hand wrist cocked at an extreme angle, and a posed shot of him with the Cardinals. A plaque for the Ron Taylor Award honored athletic-therapy students at a Toronto college who have demonstrated leadership to go with academic accomplishments. Behind glass sat a uniform signed by participants in the Joe DiMaggio Legends Game that went on for more than 10 years and raised funds for the Joe DiMaggio Children's Hospital in Fort Lauderdale. There were additional team photos of the 1964 champion Cardinals and 1969 champion Mets that Taylor played for.

Going To Bat for B.A.T.

From the time he donned his first big-league uniform, Ron Taylor knew about ex-players living out their lives struggling with financial and medical problems. That's why he supports the Baseball Assistance Team (B.A.T.). Founded in 1986 to supplant an ad-hoc players' organization, B.A.T. has provided more than $29 million in gifts from corporations, foundations, fundraisers, individuals, teams and Major League Baseball to more than 3,100 members of the "Baseball Family" who have fallen on hard times. The outreach consists of financial grants, healthcare assistance and rehabilitative counseling. "The pre-eminent organization in sports in terms of what it does for its members," the great Dodger first baseman Steve Garvey, in his 20th year on the B.A.T. board of directors, explained in 2014.

On January 21, 2014, Ron and Rona Taylor attended the 25th annual "Going to bat for B.A.T." fundraising dinner at the

New York Marriott Marquis Hotel in Times Square. A massive snowstorm may have prevented some old players from coming, but those who attended chatted and chuckled, a cheerful band of brothers.

Around 1 p.m. the Taylors entered a meeting room with small, round tables and plenty of snack food by a wall. When baseball veterans meet, memories rekindle and stories abound.

the Expos, 3–2. Relief pitchers who pick up wins are called "vultures."

"You have a good memory," McAndrew said. He kidded Taylor: "Tom Seaver said the only good throw you made in that game was when you backed up third and threw out the runner at the plate."

Ah, memories. Taylor probably did back up third, but center fielder Tommie Agee threw out a runner who tried to score from first on a single. However, Seaver had a point: Taylor yielded two hits in his inning of work.

Big Sam McDowell, a recovering alcoholic who became a substance-abuse counselor, showed up. McDowell has worked endlessly for B.A.T., counseling old-timers over "not just alcohol and drugs, but anything psychological," he admitted.

"He's a great asset to all of baseball, and he's a fine man," Taylor said.

While not hobbled as much as football retirees, elderly baseball players frequently complain of arthritis as well as knee, hip, shoulder and back problems. You might have expected a retired player to sidle up to Taylor, speak with his hands cupped over his mouth and say, "Doc, I've got this problem I want to ask you about…" Instead, old Met Ed Kranepool, his Youth of America face still recognizable, arrived to listen. "Hi, Duke," he said to Taylor. They embraced, and Kranepool listed sympathetically to Taylor's description of his PMR.

Another original Met, Al Jackson, who has more than half a century in baseball, arrived at the Taylor table. Asked how he and Taylor met, he said, "It's been a long time."

A hotel staffer with VICTOR on his nametag, asked, "What are the three wedding rings?" Nobody knew. "One for engagement, one for the wedding and one for long-suffering."

Some laughed; some groaned. Undeterred, Victor said, "How do you make a square with three lines?" Silence. Tracing a finger across the tablecloth, Victor outlined a square and then put three lines in it.

More players arrived. What a feast for baseball fans: Hall of Famer Rollie Fingers with his handlebar mustache, '69 Series star Ron Swoboda chatting with MLB TV's Harold Jackson, the old second baseman and base swiper. "Ron Taylor's one of my all-time favorite people," Swoboda said.

The great pitcher Jack Morris, a Blue Jay when Taylor was team doctor, came by. Morris's only admissions to aging were a gray goatee and glasses. Someone consoled him for missing the Hall of Fame in his 15th and final year on the ballot. "It's all good," he said. "We've got our health. That's all that matters."

At 5:30, a reception convened in a large banquet room. Tables were piled high with cheese, dumplings, pulled pork, pasta Bolognese and other treats, not to mention wine and beer. And the banquet was still to come!

Before sitting at a table to sign baseballs with Kranepool and Morris, Taylor was delighted to greet another famous ballplayer-turned-doctor, Bobby Brown, who played third base for five Yankee champions in the forties and fifties before becoming a surgeon and later American League president. "Ron's done everything," he said.

On to the banquet costing $700 apiece. Some 75 present and past baseball players and officials, including Hall of Famers Fingers, Tommy Lasorda, Orlando Cepeda and Roberto Alomar, were scattered among the tables. The first Commissioner Bud Selig Leadership Award went to Selig himself, a fervent B.A.T. supporter for some two decades. The late Michael Weiner, executive director of the players' association, received the B.A.T. Lifetime Achievement Award, which was accepted by his wife. Jimmy Rollins of the Phillies and unsigned free agent Michael Young were honored with further awards for community service.

Among players helped by B.A.T., former Pirate and Oriole outfielder Tike Redman was especially grateful. After debt mounted when his daughter Jalyn was undergoing cancer surgery and chemotherapy, B.A.T. covered the family's mortgage and utilities payments with two six-month grants. Jayln had been cancer-free for four years at the time of the dinner. "I'm very thankful," said Redman, who landed a youth-coaching job with B.A.T.'s assis-

to it.

Loyal to the game that gave him so much (and vice-versa), Taylor has no criticisms of baseball other than disagreeing with the 1973 introduction of the designated hitter and allowing for mixed feelings about pitch counts. Ask him about the "phantom" play in which a second baseman or shortstop may be allowed to touch a spot near the bag while turning a double play, he says, "They always touch the base." Criticize the umpires and he'll say, "They make the right calls. Major-league umpires are superb." He supports baseball's drug policy and is glad the players are enthusiastic about it as well.

Inevitably, he would discuss baseball with interested patients. Martin Levin, former books editor for the *Toronto Globe & Mail* and a 30-year patient of Taylor's, once asked Taylor if Bob Gibson, the fearsome Hall of Fame pitcher for the St. Louis Cardinals, was the same in the clubhouse as he was on the mound. Yes: "Focused and competitive." Was Stan Musial, whose statue sits outside the Cardinals' stadium, as virtuous and good-willed as reported? Yes.

And inevitably, Taylor was asked if there's any symbiotic relationship between baseball and medicine. Baseball is precise: hits, errors, runs, outs. Medicine is more nuanced. But both offer similar lessons. "There were times when I was discouraged [in medical school]," Taylor told the Canadian publication MD, "but those years in professional baseball taught me a lot. You can't hide your mistakes in front of a crowd, and you must learn to work under pressure. If you experience failure—and that's something every athlete experiences—you have a chance to discover something about yourself." And in an interview with Angela Parisi for U. of T Medicine, he said, "There's no substitute for passion, whatever you do. I was focused as a ball player, I was focused as an engineer, and I became focused as a doctor."

He added: "I think my experience with baseball and with injuries was valuable, but as far as diagnosis and treatment, I'd refer to a physician with a particular specialty."

If there's one major difference between his lives in the two disciplines, it's that Taylor was something of a loner in baseball but relished the human interactions in medicine.

"Ron Taylor has been my family doctor for as long as I can remember," another patient, Burl Crone, reported on Ultimate Mets Database. "The first time I required a specialist, he quizzed me on what the specialist had said, and then promptly made me an appointment for another. My whole family is in agreement that he is not only an excellent GP, but that his care in referring specialists and monitoring your care with them sets him apart. I never saw him play baseball, and he's never mentioned it. But from my experience he is an excellent physician."

"In 1981 we read an article about how Ron devised some mechanism for center fielder Rick Bosetti, whose hand was bad," said Jerry Tollinsky, an executive for a nonprofit called Boys Town Jerusalem. "I called him because my mother was having a terrible reaction from chemotherapy that was costing her the use of a hand and arm. I couldn't help but remark on how gentle he was with her. He examined her hand and created a device something like the wooden handle you see on some shopping bags. It gave her the opportunity to exercise, use her hand and take her mind off her problems in the six to eight months before she passed away.

"He looked after our whole family and a friend who had a very bad back. We all have a wonderful recollection about his care and sense of humor. We love him and wish him well."

Taylor's anonymous reviews on ratemds.com were every bit as glowing.

On a day in 2013, a man who got an appointment the same day he called was leaving the office: strictly routine chez Taylor. "Amazing—I love you guys!" the man called out. Taylor's secretary Anne Bloomfield smiled. She was having a good day. A retro

... working very hard," she said.

Rona is a tall, energetic, cheery and efficient blonde who looks younger than the 13 years she's her husband's junior. She had a pilot's license and flew planes until she decided to quit when the Taylor kids were born. "My instructor said I liked treetop flying. 'You'd have done well in the war,' he said."

In addition to making everyone she speaks to feel like the most important person in the room, Rona asks good questions and has intelligent opinions. As old family friend Don Patrick puts it, "There's no one who doesn't like Rona."

Asked about her husband's strength as a doctor, she said, "I admire him for his kindness and generous giving of time to his patients. His strength in medicine is his ability to diagnose. He says engineering makes you think analytically. Ron is slow and methodical when undertaking a task and will give you total focus until he achieves what he wants."

Turning inevitably to his personality, she added, "His dry sense of humor tends to lift spirits, and patients leave in a lighter mood."

"We met at Mt. Sinai Hospital," she continued. "He was an intern. He was very thoughtful and personable, but it took him a year to invite me to a ballgame. I had played some as a kid and I knew the gist of the game, but we weren't major-league watchers. My father was a very talented engineer but not a baseball fan.

He was trying to impress Ron, so he asked if he played with Babe Ruth."

These opposites plainly attracted. Rona's as outgoing as Ron is understated. "He's always cold, and I'm always hot!" Rona exclaimed when Ron turned on the fireplaces at their comfortable Toronto home while it was 61 degrees outside. Ron and Rona were married on September 26, 1981, the same day as Nolan Ryan's fifth no-hitter. The next year their son Drew was born. Six days later, Taylor called his sister Carole. "We're looking for Drew Taylor," he said. "Did you take him home?" Drew's brother Matthew was born in 1984.

A 6'5" left-hander who went to Michigan on a baseball scholarship, Drew spent several seasons in the minors before turning his attention to pursuit of a Ph.D. in microbiology and producing award-winning movies. Matthew, a marketer for a film company and the family wit, was born in 1984.

At Home with the Taylors

"Let's make it quick," Ron Taylor, appearing busy and serious, told a visitor to his home in October 2013. "I've got an appointment with the mayor." Toronto's mayor at the time was world-famous for being videotaped using crack.

A contented, somewhat bemused presence at his house in Toronto one afternoon in October of 2013, Taylor watched pro football on television, scowling at the hot-dog celebrations.

Identifying with Eloise, the eight-year-old pug owned by his son Matthew and Matthew's fiancée Claire Peace-MacConnell, he said, "You learn a lot from that dog. How to adapt. She's almost blind but she gets along by feel and seeing shadows. Eloise is a wonder dog."

There are framed aphorisms on the walls. "Thoughts become words. Words become actions. Actions become character. Character is everything." (Source unknown) "A friend is someone who understands your past, believes in your future, and accepts you today just the way your are." (Proverbs)

Taylor's son Drew dropped over. As a former ballplayer about to get his PhD in microbiology, he has a career arc similar to his father's. "I used to watch games with Dad, and he would ask me,

'What are you going to throw next?' At a very early age I was thinking about pitch selection and setting batters up."

In his kid bedroom, Drew has photos of broadcaster Bob Uecker and pitcher David Wells. "When Drew first started playing, a lot of his teammates wanted to come to the house to meet a major leaguer," Rona told Bob Elliott, author of The Northern Game: Baseball the Canadian Way. "It was quiet with the boys

der a different name) where Ron won his first game as a minor leaguer. "Dad let me know right off that you need to take care of your other passions." Drew said. "Baseball is so uncertain you can't count on it as a lifetime career."

That was good advice. After Drew rejected a $200,000 signing bonus from the Atlanta Braves and a $150,000 offer from the Blue Jays to attend Georgia Tech in 2001, he pitched only 9 1/3 innings and transferred to Michigan. He went 9–1 and was elected the team's Most Valuable Pitcher and Big Ten Pitcher of the Year, but made only one start in 2004 before tendinitis halted his junior season. Drew played some A-ball in the Blue Jays and Phillies organizations but lost too much in his fastball after Tommy John surgery to have a future in baseball.

Fortunately, Drew had been reading science books and watching nature shows from an early age. "One of Dad's good friends, Dr. Allan Gross, helped me and Matthew with a surgical science project. When I finished it, I said, 'I want my future to be in medicine.' Matthew said, 'I don't want my future to be in medicine.'" He went into entertainment and marketing.

In addition to his coursework, Drew produced a documentary called Our Man in Teheran that won an award at the Toronto International Film Festival. Without mentioning Argo, which focused on American heroism, Our Man fleshes out the Canadian assistance to the Americans who escaped from the embassy takeover in 1979. Drew traveled in the U.S. and Europe to pro-

mote the film. He sees his future as a movie producer and medical
consultant. (He subsequently did an award-winning short on his
father.)

Matthew and Claire arrived and entered the dining room,
dangerously close to each other. Matthew has his father's Welsh
wit. When the family was driving to a private school interview,
Matthew, then in Grade Four, said, "I sure hope Dad doesn't
blow this for me." The Taylors sat down with the headmaster,
who noticed that Matthew was looking at a picture of the Maple
Leafs on the wall. "Do you like hockey?" the headmaster asked.
"Yes." "Do you want to be a player?" "Oh, no, I want to own
the team."

In his old bedroom, Matthew has pictures of Jerry Koosman,
Mickey Mantle and Ron Taylor. At prestigious Upper Canada
College, an international baccalaureate high school, Matthew
made a short film about the basketball team that was shown at
assembly. He majored in film studies at Queens University and
has done marketing for several film companies that seem to buy
and get bought by each other. He was currently at VVS, a Montreal film company that has a Toronto office. "He always makes
the cut," Rona said. Claire is an entertainment publicist for a
film distribution company. To answer the inevitable question,
yes, Matthew had an integral role in Drew's documentary. "He
ended up securing distribution through Entertainment One Films
(EONE), which was what really got the ball rolling," Drew said.

Matthew and Claire are big-time baseball fans who frequently use Ron's tickets to Blue Jays games. "When Matthew was
eight, he and Ron went down to the Joe DiMaggio Legends Game
in Fort Lauderdale," Rona remembered. "I said, 'Ron, don't you
ever let him out of your sight,' and 'Matthew, I want you to call
every day.' So I got a call from Matthew. He said, 'Can't talk now,
we have to meet the girls.' I didn't realize it at the time, but they
were the 'girls' that 'A League of Our Own' was based on."

Matthew certainly inherited his father's chutzpah. Ron told
him not to ask for Joe DiMaggio's autograph because he didn't
sign. Matthew stood before him, program in hand. "Don't worry,
Matthew, let me sign that for you," DiMaggio said.

Matthew: "The first time we went to Shea Stadium for a reunion, there was a sea of people who knew my father. That was
the first time I saw him as a baseball player. When we went to the
Baseball Assistance Team (B.A.T.) fund-raising dinner, people de-

scended on him for autographs. I said, 'Gee, Dad, they're treating you like a hero!'"

"Dad and I visited a Mennonite farm in Alberta when he was managing in a semipro league," Drew said. "And the security guy at the gate says, 'You don't happen to be Ron Taylor?' They know him everywhere."

"We still get letters from the Mennonites." Ron said.

Update: He gave a short, tactful toast.

Despite his segue into medicine and family, Taylor has never forsaken baseball. During his year of taking catch-up courses in subjects like organic chemistry to qualify for medical school — "the toughest thing I've ever had to do" — Taylor broke stride to attend a 30th reunion Old Timers Day of the original 1962 Mets at Shea Stadium. According to one account, the ovation for him was exceeded only by those for Casey Stengel, Willie Mays, Joe DiMaggio and Yogi Berra. It was indeed like old times: a brotherhood still intact. The players stayed at the New York Athletic Club and Taylor, Tug McGraw and Jerry Koosman were inseparable. "I might be able to name 10 doctors in my graduating class and perhaps 15 engineers. But I can name all my World Series teammates, both with the Mets and the Cardinals. The pressures we went through … When you win championships like those, you're like brothers for life. That's how we are; we're all brothers."

Taylor thought pitchers will eventually wear batting helmets or high-tech headgear — some were already donning skullcaps or cap lining in spring training of 2014 on an experimental basis — to protect themselves from liners to the cranium. Catchers are starting to as well, since they're getting dinged by foul tips to the mask and the bats of hitters following through on their swings with arms extended.

"With the progress of diagnostic ability from the tools they're using now, accurate assessments and treatment have improved," Taylor said. "When I was playing, we had no MRIs for soft-tissue injuries. We had good trainers, but the tools they had weren't up to what happened now."

An MRI, or magnetic resonance imaging, is a medical technique that assesses the body's anatomy and function. MRI scanners pass over patients, using magnetic fields and radio waves to form images that isolate diseases and injuries that weren't easily detected before the procedure.

"The main thing is the increase of scientific training and sophisticated diagnostic tools," Taylor went on. "Players realize the importance of staying in shape for their whole career, because it's a lucrative profession."

"Today's game is very different," Taylor went on. "Players have scientific assessment and conditioning programs. They do controlled weight lifting scientifically. I didn't lift weights at all. There are machines that measure speed, how pitches break and what kinds of motion put the most pressure on arms. By the time they reach the major leagues, players know about the best programs. That's what they have spring training for. If there's a downside, a lot of players come back too soon from injuries and re-injure themselves. That's something you have to monitor closely.

"When I played, there was no Tommy John surgery." Also known as ulnar collateral ligament reconstruction, the treatment involves taking a tendon from another part of the body, usually the wrist or forearm, and grafting it into an elbow to replace a torn ligament. The surgery was first performed by the late Frank Jobe on left-handed pitcher Tommy John, a spring training teammate of Taylor's in the Cleveland organization. "A gentleman, well respected," Taylor said of John. And a surgical success story who won 288 games.

"The players now are big investments when they have multi-year contracts, so they aren't rushed back from injuries," Taylor said. "The game's medical care is now much more scientific and accurate. There's better training and better trainers. Every trainer has access to a computer, and every trainer sits in the dugout.

Now they have head trainers, assistant trainers, strength-and-conditioning trainers: a whole team of them.

"For conditioning, treatment and rehabilitation, the most important person is the trainer. Trainers have a college or university degree. They give pregame treatment to players recovering from injuries. They make sure all players do pregame stretch-

had an antique Valiant from the Sixties that I drove to the hospital. When he was in town managing, I drove Joe Torre to the hotel after the game and he said with some concern, 'How are you doing? How's the practice coming along?' I didn't know what year that car was. Rona got it from her father."

Noting the hot weather after the previous day's chill, Taylor observed, "It goes right from winter to summer here." Doggedly, he began driving south to the sports-medicine clinic he ran two days a week at Mount Sinai Hospital. "He's known for slow driving," Gross said. "I used to say that when we drove to the ballpark pedestrians would pass us."

At his glacial pace, Taylor gave a leisurely tour through the city. Toronto is an Indian word for "the meeting place" that superseded the short-lived, British-inspired City of York. With its substantial media presence (four daily newspapers!), lively business community and prominent hospitals, Toronto could lay claim as Canada's First City. The late *Sports Illustrated* great Ron Fimrite described Toronto as Canada's "gray lady," a perception underscored by the brick and stone buildings of the Ontario Parliament and the University of Toronto that glided by Taylor and his passenger. After fires devastated some neighborhoods, the city council banned wood as a building material. There's a stark change when you approach the downtown business, with its glass office buildings and condos. Torontonians like to think of their city as a less expensive New York. By way of example, they cite the fact that people interested in seeing the Henry Moore sculptures at the Art Gallery of Ontario can park across the street for $2.25.

If the U.S. is a melting pot, Toronto is a mosaic. Asked about ethnicity, a hyphenated American will say, "I'm an American," while a Torontonian will say, "I'm Greek" or "I'm Irish." With more than 100 different languages and dialects spoken there, Canada's largest city is one of the most multicultural cities in North America.

Taylor maneuvered into a garage parking space, backing in and out several times before satisfying himself. Walking into Mt. Sinai Hospital, he saw someone talking on a cell phone while taking the escalator down and marveled, "It's amazing how they handle those things." At the sports-injury desk on the 11th floor, he kidded two receptionists, "Are you in good moods today"?

His patients at the S.C. Cooper Family Sports Medicine Clinic always seemed to leave in good moods. When he was in medical school, Taylor met Syd Cooper, a prominent civil engineer who built much of the city's infrastructure, worked on the St. Lawrence Seaway and built many of Ontario's 400 highways. A sponsor of the Leaside junior baseball league, Cooper provided start-up funding for the clinic's 1979 opening. "He's like the second Chester Dies in my life," Taylor told Bob Elliott, referring to the Cleveland Indians scout who discovered him.

Because he had just signed on as team doctor for the Toronto Blue Jays, Taylor wanted some quick training in sports medicine. "The Cooper family was very supportive of my interests and changed my life. I knew enough to surround myself with experienced, competent and friendly people. It may have helped that I had been an athlete."

Having been injured, Taylor could pick up on sciatica or tendinitis in his patients. Taylor treated about 3,000 injuries a year. Serving people who have experienced athletic injuries and got word-of-mouth recommendations from past clients, his clinic provided experienced assessments by general practitioners, plastic surgeons, orthopedic specialists and physiotherapists. Typically, a patient saw a physiotherapist who made a finding and a recommendation. Taylor reviewed the case and decided whether future care might involve X-rays, other procedures and appointments with surgeons. Taylor also typically included taking a patient history, diagnosing the problem and beginning a rehabilitation program. Perhaps the best feature of the clinic was that it treated pa-

̴̴̴̴ ̴̴̴̴ ̴̴̴̴ ̴̴̴̴ ̴̴̴̴ ̴̴̴̴ ̴̴̴̴ ̴̴̴̴ ̴̴̴̴ ̴̴̴̴ ̴̴̴̴ ̴̴̴̴ ̴̴̴̴ ̴̴̴̴ with ankle movements and using leg weights, or standing on one foot with eyes closed. The patient thanked the physio for effective treatment.

Taylor confirmed the treatment and the diagnosis: stretching, icing and exercises with a Theraband brace, a stretchy, rubberlike elastic used against resistance, for chronic sprained ankle. "Dr. Taylor has really been wonderful," the patient said. "He has a great manner of assessment."

A man entered and gave the physiotherapist a brief history of his injury. He fell on his shoulder while skiing. The shoulder hurt for a while, and then the pain subsided. But a couple of weeks later, while preparing for a golf trip, he couldn't extend his arm upward. He tried strengthening, acupuncture, and laser treatment.

The physiotherapist assessed his strength and range of motion in his arms and shoulder. Taylor came in. "Three years ago I was in here, had a knee problem; and you introduced me to Dr. John Cameron [an orthopedic surgeon]," the patient said. "It worked! Thanks!"

Taylor manipulated his arm. "He's lost some internal rotation," he said. "Actually, it's not too bad. He has good range of motion."

The staff felt there was a small tear in the rotator cuff, which consists of three shoulder muscles. With stretching and Theraband use, the patient might not need surgery; but Taylor ordered an X-ray that evening. There was to be a follow-up with Taylor and Cameron within a week: the rapid diagnosis and quick treatment for which the clinic is known.

A third patient hurt his knee cycling about six months before and saw some improvement after visiting a physiotherapist. "She had me doing a specific stretch," he said, demonstrating by putting his left leg onto a table and reaching down to touch his right foot on the ground. There's an imbalance in the hip that causes pain all the way down the (IT) band from the hip and affects the knee.

The IT band (aka iliotibial band) is defined by Wikipedia as "a thick band of fascia [connective tissue] on the outside of the knee, extending from the outside of the pelvis, over the hip and knee, and inserting just below the knee." When the band becomes inflamed, it causes knee pain. IT Band Syndrome is especially prevalent among runners, hikers, bikers and weight lifters.

Taylor and the physiotherapist diagnosed a possible cartilage tear or treatable arthritis. An X-ray was ordered of the bone that might show a shadow of the cartilage. If pain persisted more than a few weeks, the patient would get an assessment by an orthopedic surgeon and a possible MRI that makes the tissue visible. But the patient was free to resume limited cycling, with Advil before and ice afterward.

"I called randomly and got here in a week," the patient said. "Phenomenal. The speed you can get seen and processed is amazing."

Each case had its own fascination. A woman arrived with knee problems. "Both knees click, and I jump out of my skin," she said. Retired at 59, she had resisted making an appointment. "I don't like four-letter words: rest, work," she added.

The physiotherapist carefully examined her knees. Taylor entered the area. "How's the elbow?" he asked. "Just kidding."

Actually, some patients came in complaining about one part of the body, only to discover that the issue is elsewhere. "Do you go up and down stairs?" Taylor asked the patient.

"I walk backward up a steep hill."

"That can be dangerous."

After examining the patient, Taylor said, "You've been favoring your legs [to protect the knees]. The stronger muscles are pulling the legs to the sides." A strengthening program for the inner thighs was ordered along with X-rays. The diagnosis: chondromalacia patellae, aka "runner's knee," which consists of pain from irritation of the cartilage under the kneecap—with possible osteo-

...... one side of the knee collapsed.

The medical staff diagnosed possible torn meniscus and with Taylor's approval referred the patients to further expert care from an orthopedic surgeon. She might need surgery, Taylor confided.

Other patients who were not present at the clinic freely testified to Taylor's skills. Bob Johnston, born in Lachine, Quebec, is a partner and vice president of marketing for Wanted! Sound + Picture, a company that does music, voice direction, production for commercials, television shows, and animated series. He is also a serious athlete who has competed in golf, baseball and semipro hockey.

"He was my physician for about 10 years and has treated me for shoulder, knee and arm problems," Johnston said. Asked to describe recent treatment, he cites a torn tendon in his left wrist suffered when he took a hard golf swing. "He referred me to a surgeon who ordered an MRI for assessment. After that, it was icing and light weights (typically about three pounds), nothing that would jar the wrist. I had a brace on it for a while, but not too long. He wanted to get the muscle functioning properly again.

"When I shook hands with Ron, it reminded me of my father, who was 6'4" with hands like catcher's gloves," he continued. "I call Ron a gentle giant. He's so good at the way he deals with people. His demeanor's like the old bedside manner: gentle with approach, thorough with analysis. He spends time with you and explains anatomy to you. Not your typical doctor. He's the guy to see with any kind of sports injury. As far as I'm concerned, he can do it forever."

Old buddy Don Patrick, the retired Houston surgeon who treated Taylor when he was playing for Houston, visited the clinic with Taylor on trips to Toronto. "He always put on gloves, was thoughtful and considerate and never trivialized what he saw," Patrick said. "Sometimes a patient had an angle"—say, wanted to invent an injury to stay home from work—"but he didn't discriminate or make people feel uncomfortable. I've seen orthopedists treat people brutally to make sure they were in pain, but Ron didn't behave like that. He'd say, 'O.K., this is what you've got. This is what we'll do. It'll take time, but you'll be fine.' That's the way I tried to handle things."

In an e-mail, Patrick admitted to some surprise. "When I flew to Toronto and watched him examine sports-medicine cases in his clinic, I realized that he indeed had a rare talent as a thoughtful doctor seeing patients with troubling physical ailments involving their musculoskeletal system. It is easy to hurt patients (not necessarily harm them) by doing a complete and thorough exam of the painful sites. As I watched him, he listened carefully, put on gloves, then gently moved the joints and muscles that were the primary complaint. He was exceptionally supportive and thoughtful to examine the patient thoroughly, while causing the least discomfort. I saw the vast change from the role of the professional athlete he was to the concerned and gentle healer than he became. He knew exactly how to feel and move painful joints, gathering clinical information while causing the least aggravation of symptoms by too vigorous a hands-on evaluation. He was concise and confident in his clinical skills even though he was a newly-minted doctor. I expect some of the rough-and-tumble medical exams he got as a player modified his procedures in palpating and moving painful joints and muscles. I was proud of how quickly he had learned how to become a gentle and thorough healer while causing the least anxiety and pain while was gathering valuable medical information. I was mildly distressed that I had ill-advised him not to undertake the role of a sports medicine career.

"He convinced me in just a few minutes that he had made the right professional decision by knowing himself better than I did. I continue to be a fan of him not only as a stopper with no qualms about throwing hard fastballs at opponents, hoping they couldn't escape the pain of his brusque brush back, but had the personality and caution of a Healer when he changed his roles. I am very thrilled that h~ i~~~~~~ ~ ~~~~~ ~i~~~ ~ ~~~~~~ ~~~

~~~~~~ ~~~~~~~ ~~~ ~~~~~~~ ~~ ~~~~~~~ ~~ emergencies in 2010. He remained an emeritus Jays' doctor.

"Since I was competent and had played baseball and gone back to medical school, Ken Carson, the Blue Jays' trainer at the time, mentioned me to Peter Bavasi, the general manager. Being a former player may have been helpful. There was a faint pulse."

"Ron had the sensibility to handle players," Bavasi said. "I thought, 'You know what? He doesn't need to be an orthopedist.'" And so Taylor became the prototype of the modern team doctor: a generalist who can recommend specialists.

"I had just finished my residency, so I recruited Allan Gross and other specialists from different disciplines, so I had competent coverage from an orthopedic as well as a medical standpoint," Taylor said. "My main strength was getting people like Allan Gross to treat the players."

"Being a former player helps me relate with the current players, and the problems they have," Taylor told Ross Foreman of *Sports Collectors Digest*. "I have empathy for what they're going through—the highs, the lows, the injuries, the heartaches, etc." The most common injuries he treated Blue Jays for were upper extremity: hands, elbows and shoulders.

It wasn't just Taylor's credibility as an ex-player that impressed the Blue Jays. Pat Gillick, who was director of player personnel and later general manager of the Blue Jays during Taylor's tenure there, said, "He cared not only for the players but for their wives and families. He was a doctor for the whole family. His commitment was unbelievable. He surrounded himself with a lot of experts and had access to people, no matter what the field. If he couldn't treat a problem himself, he had no ego whatsoever. If it was best to refer the patients to someone else, he'd do it. He had the interests of his patients always in his mind."

Sometimes visiting players and team executives would seek him out. "When Pat Gillick joined the team, he came to my office feeling lousy," Bavasi said. "He thought he'd picked up the flu or something worse on a trip to the Caribbean. We walked over to Ron's office. He gave him some appropriate medication. When I got fired and came up with an infectious disease in 1981, Ron got me to the right people at Mt. Sinai."

If Taylor said he just made recommendations to specialists, he might have been a trifle modest. It's reasonable to speculate that his personal experience in baseball helped him to diagnose problems. A player may come to a team doctor with soreness in the knee and be logically diagnosed with knee sprain, only to discover later that he has a tibia fracture; a former player might make the right diagnosis. As a former pitcher, he says he was able to diagnose throwing injuries more quickly than other team doctors. For such a modest man who usually credits the doctors he whom he referred players to, that's quite an admission. Nonetheless, he refuses to cite a case of his unique insight. "We worked as a team," he says, citing the two surgeons on staff.

Some ailments are almost impossible to detect. Neck and shoulder pain and finger numbness can result from Thoracic Outlet Syndrome, which occurs when the blood vessels or nerves compress between the scapula, aka collarbone, and first rib. "Because there's no pain involved and a lot of the cases are not dramatic, Thoracic Outlet Syndrome may be the most undetected pitching problem out there," Texas Rangers' trainer Jamie Reed, who worked rehabbing four different players who had surgery for TOS, told journalist Peter Gammons. "It's something the industry may look into deeper."

"With the progress of diagnostic ability from the tools they're using now, accurate assessments and treatment have improved," Taylor said. "When I was playing, we had no MRIs or diagnostic ultrasounds for soft-tissue injuries. We were basically told we had to take care of the injuries ourselves."

Taylor pitched Blue Jays' batting practice for more than 10

Taylor has a photo of himself sitting with a player; it's hard to tell the moundsman from the medic. He was not just one of the guys, but more than a little appreciated. "Pat and I were trying to describe him the other day," Bavasi said. "Is laconic or droll the right word? He had that semi-astonished look on his face. Players would call him weird, but they meant it as 'the most fascinating and unusual guy I've ever played with.' They meant it affectionately."

"Rona tells the story about when she and Ron visited the Cape Cod League to watch Drew pitch," Gillick said. "A woman had read in the paper that this boy was pitching and came out to see him. She introduced herself to Ron, who was very polite to her. Rona stood behind the woman and kept flashing two fingers. The woman was Ron's second wife, and he didn't recognize her!"

As much as he identified with the players, sometimes Taylor had to stand up to them. In 1989 Tony Fernandez, the Blue Jays shortstop, was struck on the right cheek by a pitch and suffered a fracture of the zygomatic bone. Fernandez asked to come off the disabled when he was eligible, but Taylor turned him down. "It's just too risky," he told MD. "Any kind of blow or violent collision could do a lot of damage to the fractured area, even with a protected helmet."

Taylor would go to spring training three or four times on weekends and travel with the team if it reached the postseason. When the Blue Jays were home, he arrived at the ballpark several hours before gametime to check the players, except when he had his Tuesday and Wednesday sports-injury clinics. Early in his Blue Jays practice, there were no MRIs, and players played through pain unless there was something drastically wrong with them. By the mid-80s, doctors were using CT scans (computer pictures developed from eX-rays) and MRIs early in a player's injury history. It was never desirable to hide injuries in the first place, and they became more difficult to hide.

Working for the Blue Jays, running a private practice and operating the clinic was such a joyride for Taylor that he never complained about sometimes working 72-hour weeks. In fact, he loved it. The club now rotates three orthopedic surgeons and several G.P.'s to home games. Home-team clinicians also treat visiting players while consulting with their club's doctors if necessary.

As the team doctor, Taylor would watch games on TV from the clubhouse in order to report quickly for emergencies. One of his concerns was treating injuries without "advertising" them and alerting opponents about a player's weakness. Taylor's toughest moments came when batters or pitchers were hit on the head. He explains the protocol:

"The first guy out is the player's team trainer. The other team's trainer may be there, too. If they need a doctor or stretcher, they'll call for it. You first have to make sure he didn't swallow his tongue. That could kill him, and you'd have to do the Heimlich Maneuver. There could be a laceration in which the player swallows blood. You apply pressure to the area and stabilize it. If there's no airway, the orthopedic may have to perform a tracheotomy.

"They stabilize the head and neck and put him on a stretcher limo to the clubhouse, and from there usually to a hospital. These things rarely happen, but when they do you have to be ready for them."

Taylor missed few games in 21 years. On this midweek day in May 2013, he was sitting in the press box at Rogers Centre watching a game. Taylor liked the sightlines and the press-box TVs that show replays.

Before the game, the coaches threw batting practice. No longer do pitchers, who might have trouble warming up and warming down often······· ··· ······ ···· T··· ···· ··

····· ·· ····· ········ ·· ···· ······ ··· ···· ·I want to thank Ron Taylor for all he's done for medicine and baseball.'

"He was an icon. Toronto? Medicine? Sports?" He pointed at Taylor.

Asked what advice he'd give today's ballplayers, Taylor said, "Maintaining your fitness year-round and keeping in shape during the off-season will give you a quicker start in the regular season. Players used to get out of shape in the Fifties and use spring training to get in shape. Now they report in shape and work on the weaknesses in their game in spring training. By the time the season starts, that's all behind them; and they're ready to go."

After 7½ innings, Taylor left a game in which the Blue Jays were thrashing the Giants. He began to muse. "I met my first wife when I was studying engineering. The marriage lasted three years. I met my second wife, an airline stewardess, in New York. Three years. My shelf life." He declined to elaborate further on the marriages.

"I've been lucky. How many guys can say they pitched almost 500 games, had an engineering degree and a doctor's degree? You had to be some kind of whacko to pull that off." A whacko who still belongs to the Ontario Society of Professional Engineers, the Major League Baseball Players' Association and the Ontario Medical Association. A whacko who was inducted into the Canadian

Baseball Hall of Fame (1985) and the Canadian Sports Hall of Fame (1993), while receiving the Order of Ontario (2006) for his medical work.

Asked about future plans, he said, "We were supposed to go to the British Isles before the PMR came up. We thought about a river cruise."

At the time, he was just musing, but early in 2014 Taylor decided to retire. "I'm 76, I've accomplished a lot of what I wanted to do, and it's time to travel," he said. "I want to go to Ireland and Wales because my parents came from there, and take a river cruise down the Danube."

First, he and other surviving members of the Cardinals' 1964 world champions got a 50th reunion tribute in St. Louis on May 26. Taylor, like each of his teammates, sat alone in the back of a car driven around Busch Stadium while a standing-room-only crowd of 47,311 cheered before a game with the Yankees. He felt like the Duke of Earl. Then he endured a June roast back home and set about closing his office and selling the building that housed it.

Finally, Ron and Rona had the luxury to hit the road, which will also include trips much closer to home than overseas. "I wish he'd already retired," Rona said during the bleak winter of 2013–14. "We could have spent February and March at spring training!"

We should spend 12 months a year celebrating Ron Taylor's life and work. "To do what he did," Tim McCarver said in Drew Taylor's documentary, "I think that's an idyllic way to live your life."

CHAPTER FIVE

Good Times Never Seemed So Good

nedy, the Vineyard more recently has become famous for the filming of the movie Jaws in 1974 and as the vacationland of presidents Clinton and Obama. The Island's fabulous beaches, ponds and lands, its twisted-oak woods and glacial cliffs are attraction enough; but the vitality of its 16,000 year-round citizens and 106,000 summer residents is staggering. There's a Film Center playing movies you'd really like to see, a cultural mecca at the Hebrew Center, the internationally famous Farm Neck Golf Club open to the public, as well as accessible experts on many a subject. Everyone wants to be there. There's no telling what you'll come across.

June 10, 2011—the night before the Martha's Vineyard Sharks of the amateur Futures Collegiate Baseball League (FCBL) open their first season against the Seacoast Mavericks from Rochester, New Hampshire.

High-level baseball on Martha's Vineyard! Not only that but high-level baseball using wooden rather than metal bats, a pleasure usually reserved for pros. But the players gathered at Zephrus restaurant in Vineyard Haven are not your grandfather's prospective major leaguers. Mostly over six feet tall, with thick necks and six-pack abs, they include pitchers who throw more than 90 miles per hour and batters who hit the ball 400 feet. All of them are collegians and most of them play baseball for three out of four seasons, with winter reserved for conditioning. There are athletes from Harvard and Brown; a surfer dude from California; players from Protestant, Catholic and Jewish backgrounds; Anglos and Latinos. They sit at tables in shorts, sneakers and T-shirts, bonding like fraternity brothers.

The Sharks will play 44 games over 51 days against the league's other teams: the Seacoast Mavericks, the Nashua (NH) Silver Knights, and the Torrington (CT) Titans, plus a few other games against nonconference opponents. Their shortest bus ride is around two and one-half hours. Major league scouts will take copious notes.

Wearing longer pants and only slightly more ample midsections, two equally accomplished club executives are beaming in an adjacent room. "This is something I wanted to do before they pour dirt on me," says Vice President of Baseball Operations Bob Tankard, a management consultant whose lengthy C.V. includes stints as head football coach at Martha's Vineyard Regional High School and principal of the West Tisbury School. He currently serves on the Tisbury School Committee, as vice chair of the Cape Cod Collaborative serving kids in need, and as a board member of Martha's Vineyard Savings Bank. "What a fine thing to do: baseball, hot dogs, affordable family entertainment, with adults paying $5 and kids $3. This is almost like the minor leagues in 1961."

Tankard motions over General Manager Jerry Murphy, who is retired from stints as a bank executive and CEO of a software company and a renewal-energy project. Murphy has coached the JV baseball team at Martha's Vineyard Regional High School. Both he and Tankard were hired by the Sharks' majority owner Chris Carminucci, whose Carminucci Sports Group operates the Torrington club and the Brockton Rox of the professional Can-Am League. Carminucci landed a five-year, rent-free lease with the school system to play at the high school's Vineyard Baseball Park. In return, the Sharks guarantee year-long maintenance of the playing grounds and by Opening Day have already spent about $250,000 to build a storage shed, pay volunteers to construct outbuildings, buy a tractor and other equipment, add bleachers and install a new watering system and underground electrical lines to upgrade the field. For their part, Tankard and Murphy have signed up some 70 sponsors. "We're the Cisco Kid and Pancho," Tankard says.

"Which is which?" Murphy says. Turning more serious, he adds, "Our success will depend on whether we're competitive and

versity in Texas with outtasight junior-college stats from the previous season. "Didn't you hit something like .750 last year?" Murphy asks him.

"Something like that," Autrey murmurs.

"And wasn't your on-base percentage about .850?" Tankard suggests.

"I guess."

"I want all these kids to have a great time, win some games and improve a part of their game," says head coach Ted Currle, whose Norton (MA) High School team won the Division 3 state title in 2010.

Chosen from among more than 200 candidates with the help of a scouting bureau and college coaches, at least 13 of the 24 Sharks must live in New England or play for area schools by league fiat. The players and the team kick in $300 apiece to pay the families who put them up—after the hosts undergo a criminal-record check. The players sign a disciplinary sheet promising that under-21 athletes will avoid bars and everyone will smile, sign autographs, appear at functions, help maintain the field, perform up to 20 hours of community service and stay out of trouble. Some will also teach baseball at Murphy's baseball camp for $20 an hour.

Opening Day

June 11, 2011. During a break from warm-ups, the team's only Vineyard resident, Tad Gold of Vineyard Haven, fields questions in the dugout. The son of Wally, a carpenter, and Melissa, a bookkeeper, he is wearing his pants high, exposing black hose almost to the knee like old-fashioned ballplayers. "Lacrosse takes a lot of [high-school] players from baseball," says Gold, a sophomore at Beverly's Endicott College. "I just kept at it. The Sharks could mean a lot for youth programs and more players in high school."

Gold himself could mean a lot for Vineyard baseball. The nice quarter-Jewish lad is a 15th-generation Vineyarder on his mother's side, with antecedents dating back to the Mayhews and Leonards and Chief Sengekontacket, or so say relatives. "He took a post-graduate year at Bridgton Academy in Maine," says his grandmother Cynthia Schilling, a trim, white-haired woman wearing a Sharks' cap, a Black Dog T shirt, blue jeans and sneakers. "They couldn't say enough about his athletic prowess in hockey and baseball. He'd never run track before, but he was the fastest runner they ever had at Bridgton."

She's just getting started. "He was as comfortable with his great-grandparents as he is with his peers. We have a photo of him with his 96-year-old great-grandmother when he was 18. He's looking down at her, and she's looking up at him. 'I love you, Tad,' she's saying. 'I love you, Connie,' he tells her."

Some of Gold's teammates sign balls; other play catch with a little kid on the sidelines. First baseman Anthony Boix of Tennessee Wesleyan College bops to music over the P.A. "You gotta dance, man," he says. "You gotta have fun at the ballpark."

French-surnamed Boix, who has a father of Cuban ancestry and a mother of Dominican and Peruvian roots, converses with Jeremy Matos, who cites Puerto Rican, French and Turkish antecedents. "I don't speak Spanish, but I understand my grandmother when she speaks it," Boix says.

"That's more than I can do," Matos says.

By the 5 p.m. start, established that early because of the lightless field and the need for visiting teams to make the last ferry, fevered preparations are complete. Hannah Schley, the 24-year-old club president, grins over the purple coating she has applied to the inside of the dugouts. Ads for local businesses like Vineyard Cash & Carry and Our Market adorn the outfield fences. Head coach Currle lays down chalk on the first-base line. General Manager Murphy staffs a concession stand. You can't make this kind of

minute, a race among youngsters and the mascot Sharky (you can imagine who finishes last).

"I called some minor-league stadiums to see what works," pastor Jeff Winter of Faith Martha's Vineyard Church, who supervises on-field promotions, says. "I have about 40 different things to use, some of which I made up. My favorite is asking Sharks players questions about Martha's Vineyard." He paused and smiles. "They know a lot about baseball."

With the Sharks trailing 1–0 in midgame, Gold reaches first on a strike-three passed ball; two teammates get on to load 'em up; and the ebullient Boix triples everyone home. The Sharks go on to win, 6–1. You doubtless noticed that the Vineyard kid scored the team's first run of the season.

An overflow crowd of about 2,100 leaves well entertained. During the following weeks, the Sharks stage special promotions for groups they hope will be repeat customers: the Boys & Girls Club, Camp Jabberwocky, Martha's Vineyard Savings Bank, Island Elderly Housing, volunteer firemen, families, even dog owners. Each game's guests get wristbands guaranteeing them free food. For youngsters with short attention spans there's a Kids Zone down the left-field line with a sandbox, a bouncy castle and a hoop-shooting apparatus. People dodging the sun can repair to a 2,000-square-foot tent area. There's a "shark launch" using toy fish and slingshots. Kids linger behind the stands because if you catch a ball, you can turn it in at a concession stand for a free cookie or some other dessert. Because home games are played on high-school land, smoking and alcohol are verboten. Talk about family entertainment!

Good Sports

Anticipating some burnout, Ted Currle girds for the time in early July when "they've been playing since February." Indeed, games follow in which the pitchers are so wild they allow eight runs on only six hits, days when the P.A. plays "rally" music when the other team is batting. But there always seem to be at least a few hundred people at the park, with visitors from places like Georgia, Tennessee, Nebraska, South Carolina and, believe it or not, Mongolia. The fans chant for the Sharks even when they're behind by six runs with two out in the ninth. Good humor is always the winner. "What time is it in Vancouver?" asks Ken Goldberg, who broadcasts some Shark games on cable TV. Then he answers his own question: "Twenty minutes past Luongo," referring to the Vancouver goalie beaten by the champion Boston Bruins.

The players relish their summer. "They're so polite," says Joan Dunayer, owner of Martha's Vineyard Real Estate and host for catcher Anthony Corona. "Anthony always hugs me and says, 'Good morning, Joan,' and 'Good night, Joan.'"

"When we get a day off, we'll go to South Beach," Gold says, apparently speaking for the entire team.

You want a feel-good story? In his junior and senior years of high school in Southbury, Connecticut, pitcher Adam Cherry raised enough money on behalf of Strike Out Hunger to provide 25,000 meals. "He's a good kid, a good boy," says his mother Mary Anne. "Not that any mother would say that."

As the tourist season starts, there's more than just baseball to keep the faithful coming. Volunteers launch T-shirts into the stands. The sack race always seems to involve a tall boy, a small boy and a gremlin-sized girl. One kid is seen with four foul balls he has caught after scouting the busiest locations.

"The ball boys are so cute!" Hannah Schley says. One of them goes to work with the remnants of a blue Slurpee covering his mouth. Another runs out with the coaches to comfort Corona after he takes a foul tip off his hand.

Because buses cost about $1,500 per round trip, the Sharks cannot afford to stay overnight on the road. Even when they have two successive road games, they get up early, take the bus to Torrington, Nashua or Rochester, play the game, get back on the bus,

models. In the little free time he has, Corona works as a bouncer at the Edgartown nightclub Nectars.

A Midsummer's Daydream

July 8, 2011. Though some players are fighting a stomach bug, the second-place Sharks nonetheless field a team to play first-place Nashua on July 8. (The top two teams will qualify for a best-of-three championship playoff in early August.) Fighting injury rather than sickness, Jeramy Matos, who has café-au-lait skin, a sculpted fringe beard à la David Ortiz, and a nose that meanders like the Nile, has been hitting like Albert Pujols. In fact, the Cardinal star is his role model. Major leaguers have been restricting the strides with their front foot or eliminating them altogether. "I'm a big fan of The Mental Keys to Hitting by Harvey Dorfman," Matos says. "[A stride] makes your eyes drop. See the ball; know your strength; keep your head still. Pujols especially. That's why he's called The Machine."

Around 4 p.m., Matos repairs to the right-field stands and pulls his pants down to just above his knees. Wearing boxer-like undershorts, he's preparing his ailing legs for physical therapy.

Susan Sanford, a gum-chewing blonde in flip-flops, jeans, sleeveless blouse, hoop earrings, and sunglasses perched atop her head, approaches. A licensed physical therapist, licensed acupuncturist and certified sports-medicine acupuncturist, she applies gel to the quadriceps, covers it with a pad attached to a small electrical box in her hand, and uses low-frequency stimulation over specific points on the muscle. The muscle jumps. "The idea is to twitch and stimulate muscles to recovery," she says. "When you cause an involuntary muscle contraction, you're pressing the neurological reset button to restore function, reduce pain and eliminate spasms."

Music chosen by the players blares over the P.A. "Good time," Jeramy sings to it, "boogie." A rap song whose most innocuous word may be "bitch" follows to Matos's dismay. "You never used to hear the B word," he says. (Cleaner music will play when the fans show up.)

"I'm really sore," says Matos. "I've had two strained hamstrings for a month. It sucks. I can't sprint. The only way to deal with it is to take time off, but…"

He doesn't need to finish the sentence: time off is not an option when you aren't crippled by injury and you're trying to impress pro scouts over a short season.

Sanford massages his quadriceps muscles and instructs Matos to do a quad stretch. He grabs his right instep and swings it to his butt, knee facing the ground. "I couldn't do that this morning," Matos says.

Before releasing him, Sanford applies two long stretches of pink Kinesio® Tex Tape covered by two horizontal strips to each quad, giving him support without reducing flexibility or circulation. "I don't feel it when I play," Matos says of his pain. "I play through it. I have to."

"All right!" Sanford says. "Knock 'em dead! Hit 'em out of the park!"

The game begins with a fog creeping over the center-field fence. Ah, Vineyard fog: not too hot, not too cold, accompanied by a comforting little breeze. The idea of fog is so resonant that Carl Sandburg wrote the poems "Fog" and "Fog Portrait" about it.

As cleanup hitter, Matos strikes out on a breaking ball in the dirt his first time up. But on his second at bat, he picks on a hanging curve and hits a three-run homer over the left-field fence. He taps batting helmets with the two base runners when he crosses the plate. Later he drives in a run with a single. Give Sanford an assist for getting him in playing shape.

to the Sharks when Garrett Autrey is hurt, starts in left. He and Matos are longtime friends. In fact, Matos's father Ralph recommended Goodman to the Vineyard staff when the vacancy opened.

A muscular little guy, Goodman steps in and assumes a stance that begins with a lean backward as if he were evading a bully's fists. "I don't know where he got that," his father says appreciatively. "He got that from himself."

Goodman, who is listed at 5'10" but stands 5'8½", gets a single and also hits a sharp grounder that the pitcher blindly stabs at and knocks down before throwing in time to first, has hit .353 at Miami-Dade Junior College, where major league teams drafted five of his teammates. "He's our little prospect," his father says. "I don't know if he's anybody else's."

A catcher in the Cincinnati Reds' farm system before a career-ending injury in A-ball, David Goodman supplies knowing commentary during the game while Lisa offers popcorn to a new acquaintance. The game is called off because of fog with the score 5–5 in the eighth inning, but everyone leaves well entertained. (The Sharks will win when the game resumes on July 20.)

The Big Picture

In baseball, the only constant is change. On July 12, Sanford rolls her eyes when asked about Matos's condition. After the game starts, he runs stiffly to first on a groundout. Pretty soon he may be used as a pitcher when he isn't lumbering along as the designated hitter.

"See that speed?" Bob Tankard says after a new player, Calvin Graves, legs out an infield hit. "He must have gone down there in four steps!"

There's growing attention now on shortstop Robbie Zinsmeister from Indiana University of Pennsylvania. He not only has good hands afield but also is among the team leaders in every important offensive category, including stolen bases.

Blond and pleasant, Zinsmeister deflects attention from himself. "I'm from Hatfield in eastern Pennsylvania, and I go to school in the western part of the state," he says. "People are different there." He chuckles. "They say 'pop' instead of 'soda.'"

Asked to explain his summer success, he says, "Maybe the pitching is tougher in my college league." Maybe, but he was also an all-star for the Quakertown Blazers in the Atlantic Collegiate Baseball League the previous summer.

By the sizzling Friday night of July 22, the real world begins closing in on the Sharks. They're now in third place, with only a week and a half left. It's 93 degrees at game time. "If I go 6 for my next 6, I'm going home!" Boix shouts to hoots from his teammates.

Not a chance. There are no unions or agents for summer players, and no one wants to build up a bad reputation. When a coach tells you to jump, you ask him, "How high?"

Calvin Graves has a hamstring problem and decides to leave the team to recuperate before fall practice at New Hampshire's Franklin Pierce University. Matos sticks it out, although he can't bend his knee behind him at more than a 90-degree angle. Nonetheless, he repairs to the batting cage, where a teammate lobs balls underhand and Matos hits them with only his left hand on the bat.

Darren Harrison-Panis, a part owner and Sharks representative on the FCBL board of directors, originated the idea of an FCBL with a team on the Vineyard. It's no surprise that he looks at the big picture when he's asked to evaluate the season. "We're averaging almost 700 fans a game," he says. "It's become part of everyone's summer tradition. When people come here, they go to

and say, "This is the year so-and-so came of age as a ballplayer en route to the majors?" That's certainly the goal of every Shark. On Monday, July 25, eight Sharks head to the Brockton ballpark for a Scouts Day. Matos, Zinsmeister, Corona, Boix, and pitchers Zach Rafferty, Jay Swinford and Ryan Morris make the trip, along with Eric Jensen, who is subbing for the injured Rosario. Working out before representatives from 18 major-league teams and two more from the Major League Scouting Bureau, the eager eight and players from other FCBL teams take infield practice, show off outfield and pitching arms, take batting practice and play a simulated game with hitting and pitching but no base running.

"Scouts are strange guys," Tankard says. "They'll look at you like this" — he faces forward while looking out the corner of his eyes — "because they don't want you to notice. But when they get back to the office, the phone starts ringing."

If Robbie Zinsmeister, considered the best all-around Shark, is disturbed that he didn't get much visible attention on Monday, he doesn't show it on Tuesday. Zinsmeister's eighth-inning homer gives the Sharks a 2–1 win over Torrington. It's win-or-else time. The Sharks are three games behind Nashua and Torrington, who have identical first-place records, with just seven games to go.

The Sharks win on Wednesday, and then win in spectacular form on Thursday, when Matos hits a three-run homer in the first, followed by solo shots in the third and fifth. But a walkoff homer in the ninth by—whom else?—Zinsmeister gives the Sharks a 7–6 win over the Silver Knights. Martha's Vineyard is now one and a half games behind league-leading Nashua and a game behind Torrington.

Then, after some tough losses, August 2 arrives with the Sharks trailing Torrington by two games; and two games, both with the Titans, remaining on their schedule. That means the Sharks will have to beat Torrington twice, then beat them again in a one-game playoff. The players are remarkably relaxed, willing even to talk about their futures. "I've worked hard on my running," says Corona, "running with a parachute in the winter and trying to perfect my jump off first. There aren't many fast catchers, and I'm glad I've stolen a few bases this summer. I've always looked up to pros like Jason Kendall."

Wouldn't you know, a few hours later Boston catcher Jarrod Saltalamacchia pinch-runs for Jason Varitek and races home for the winning run against Cleveland?

Before the first Torrington game, the Sharks line up their Vineyard hosts, who throw baseballs to the players they house. Another good move by team management. The Sharks don't make the postseason, but not for lack of trying. Tonight's 2–1 defeat to Torrington kayoes them. But with or without the playoffs, it's a successful season. The Sharks finish with a 23–21 league record and lead the FCBL in hitting. Four players—Zinsmeister (shortstop), Matos (DH), Corona (catcher) and Jensen (utility)—make the FCBL's All-Star team, and Zinsmeister is elected the league's MVP.

"Coming up short left a bad taste in everyone's mouth, but every kid who put out showed improvement," head coach Currle says. In addition to citing players like Zinsmeister ("the full package"), Matos, Corona and Zach Rafferty who may be drafted by major-league organizations, he adds, "[Third baseman] Steve Schoettmer struggled but came to the park every day to work on his hitting and improved his average by about 100 points." Alas, the Vineyard's own Tad Gold has just 14 hits, all singles, as he struggles to pivot off his back foot. [He later improved his hitting enough to sign with the Orioles for two seasons, plus winter ball in Perth, Australia, before being released.]

A couple of hours after their last game, Sharks players Max Goodman, Anthony Corona, Eric Jensen and John Keating sit on an Oak Bluffs porch eating pizza and corn on the cob. There's no bragging, and surprisingly little talk about baseball. Unlike so

dinary individual voted the leadership award by his teammates. Corona, the son of a retired New York City cop, is majoring in education at C.W. Post College, his future in mind.

Corona dreams of landing in The Show. If the pros don't draft him, he plans to be a volunteer assistant on the C.W. Post team because the school will pay for his Master's in education. Then he'll teach history in high school (he's already researching a book on the Battle of Gettysburg) and may end his working life as a state trooper. "Not the nasty kind," he says. He's already taken the NYPD test.

"It was great playing ball on the Vineyard," he says. "The beautiful beaches, the interesting things to do." He adds his thanks to Vineyarders for their support and hospitality.

"Most college leagues are in small towns," Goodman says in further appreciation of the Island's many pleasures.

"In school it's all about winning," Jensen adds. "The coaches have to win or they'll lose their jobs. This was much more fun. The coaches let us play."

Asked about some humorous experiences, they all cite the game in which pitcher Kody Kasper tackles a mascot called Monkey Boy who is stripping at a Nashua Silver Knights game. Though the event quickly becomes a YouTube classic, the league immediately kicks Kasper off the team for misbehavior.

"Bad decision by Kody," Corona says.

"Also one of the funniest things I've ever seen in baseball," says Keating.

When a game in Nashua gets rained out, players from both teams disport themselves doing tarp slides. The Sharks spend every free day at the beach. When Matt Hegarty's little cousins pull some garter snakes out of a bag, Kaspar runs a quarter of a mile down the beach. When the kids follow him, snakes in hand, teammates swear he runs another mile.

"In baseball, you don't want to tell people your phobias," Goodman says.

On endless bus rides, players watch movies and play celebrity/ athlete guessing or card games like spades. Their longest trip takes them to a nonconference game in Oneonta, New York; and they visit the Hall of Fame in nearby Cooperstown. The bus arrives in Woods Hole around 3 a.m., several hours before the first ferry to the Vineyard. "We were sleeping on benches like monks," Corona says.

But they played like Sharks.

CHAPTER SIX

Here's To the Good Old Days

At the conclusion of every baseball storm—be it a strike or a rash of drug busts or the latest contract hassle—players and executives fall back on that old bromide: "All that really matters is what goes on between the white lines."

Well, 1983 wasn't an exceptional year between the white lines. The most memorable moment on the field concerned pine tar—specifically whether too much of it on the bat of the Royals' George Brett was sufficient cause for disallowing a game-winning home run he'd hit against the Yankees. The incident generated one of the liveliest and most interesting debates in the history of the sport. The controversy, which resulted in Brett's homer being allowed to stand, was particularly well suited to baseball, which is as much a game of talk as action. But pine tar aside, it was what happened outside the white lines that gave '83 its special flavor.

JAN. 23—The baseball season doesn't begin with the first pitch of spring training or even the first pitch of Opening Day. It begins with the annual New York Baseball Writers dinner, the first big baseball event of the year. It's a watershed in which the season past is celebrated and the season future anticipated.

For eating or entertainment, the dinner isn't much. Furthermore, it is militantly, even offensively, all-male; the word stag fairly leaps out of the invitation. So why do I attend a dinner run by such antediluvian people? Because in a strange way, they're my heroes. These cigar-chomping traditionalists represent some of the game's best instincts. There's nothing about baseball they've ever wanted to alter. Oh, sure, some things, such as segregation and low salaries, cried out for change. But baseball rules and traditions were by and large perfect as they stood in, say, 1950. In one of the game's greatest ironies, the "progressives" gave us the DH, artificial turf, indoor stadiums, expansion and most everything else that over the past two decades or so has dulled the spectacle.

FEB. 28—I have two conflicting views of spring training. The first is the traditional one—that the baseball spring is a time of rebirth and renewal. The weather is warm, the atmosphere is informal, the mood is upbeat. Every team is improved, every rookie is a phenom. In the outfield, players, their caps purposely askew, throw balls between their legs. Other players—and coaches and managers—lean over the railing and strike up conversations with fans. The scene should be frozen forever.

But I also think about players who may be coming to spring training for the last time. Age and injury have dimmed their skills. For them, it's a time of desperation, not celebration.

MARCH 21—The atmosphere at a spring training game is quite unlike that at a regular-season game. No one really cares about the result, because the starters are replaced by minor-leaguers after a few innings. The movement of people in the stands is every bit as fluid. Fans drift in, drift out, show up during the sixth inning. At Al Lang Stadium in St. Petersburg there's a celebrated hot dog vendor. When he makes his grand entrance in the third inning, fans applaud, and surprised players turn around to see what's going on. "World's worst hot dogs!" the old fellow cries out. Later he breaks into a raucous tenor and sings He's Got the Whole World in His Hands.

I watched today's game with Roger Angell, the distinguished fiction editor and baseball writer for *The New Yorker*. Roger's a sensitive and charming fellow, but he couldn't restrain himself the first time Dave Kingman, the wasted talent for the Mets, stepped to the plate. Roger stuck out his tongue, blew on it and gave Kingman the raspberry: "Btfstpk!"

"Roger!" said his wife, Carol.

"Btfstpk!"

Carol was blushing and laughing now. The Angells' 12-year-old son, John Henry, had one of those "Oh, Dad!" looks on his face.

"Btfstpk!" he bleated again, whereupon some Met fans turned around and looked nervously at him.

by formality, humor by seriousness, warmth by cold, dreams by reality. Suddenly, the red-hot rookie who wowed 'em in Florida is gaping at the sight of the mammoth stadium where the play is for keeps. Suddenly, the players must back up the boasts their manager has been making about them all March.

APRIL 13—The Red Sox-Royals game in Kansas City was delayed for an hour by rain. Inside the Boston clubhouse, the Sox played miniature golf with bats, balls and paper cups. One of the best things about baseball, Texas third baseman Buddy Bell told me a few days ago, is that, as a player, you never have to grow up. When they tired of golf, the Sox began imitating each other at the plate. Second baseman Jerry Remy, impersonator par excellence, brought down the house with his portrayal of first baseman Dave Stapleton hanging his head after hitting a pop-up.

I think ballplayers razz each other for two reasons: They've got a lot of time with nothing better to do, and they play under too much tension to take everything seriously. "You have to have very thick skin to be a ballplayer," Sox pitcher Bruce Hurst told me. While looking for a house in Boston, Hurst and his wife have been living with the Celtics' Danny Ainge, who once played baseball for the Toronto Blue Jays. "Danny and I were talking about baseball and basketball," says Hurst, who played hoops at Dixie

College in Utah. "We agreed that it's tougher to take ribbing in baseball. When you're playing with 24 other guys instead of 11, there's a greater chance someone will get under your skin."

APRIL 22—Nolan Ryan of the Astros will shoot for the career strikeout record tomorrow, but the game at the Astrodome won't come close to selling out. "I bet we only get 20,000," said Houston reliever Dave Smith. "The fans here aren't very knowledgeable about baseball. They only come out when we're winning." The Astros have been losing.

Smith unwittingly put his finger on one of the game's lingering problems. Baseball has expanded and probably will continue to expand to cities that have large, often indoor stadiums and are situated in attractive television markets. Most expansion cities also have poor baseball traditions and fans who are more likely to be taken with mascots and exploding scoreboards than good pickoff plays. In such fashion does baseball become richer—and poorer.

APRIL 27—A major discovery: There are more good guy ballplayers who work hard, love the game and hate to lose than I thought. While waiting for Ryan to set the record in his second try—he came up five strikeouts short in Houston—I sat in the press box at Montreal's Olympic Stadium with Hal Bock of the Associated Press and Henry Hecht of the New York Post. The three of us tried to create an all-star team composed of jerks—and couldn't fill the positions.

MAY 15—Art Shamsky, a broadcaster and former Met, had a thoughtful piece in *The New York Times* today about beanballs. Of all the ongoing scandals in baseball, the beanball is one of the worst. Its perpetrators can choose from among several excuses for committing the crime. "I have to have the inside of the plate," they say. Or, "I was just trying to move him back." Or, "The pitch got away from me." Or, "It's part of the game."

It used to be part of the game to call Jewish players Moe. It used to be part of the game to have no black players. It used to be part of the game for players to wear no protective headgear or catcher's equipment. Baseball discarded these idiocies but not the beanball.

MAY 25—For the last two games, I've sat at Cincinnati's Riverfront Stadium with Charles Newman, a novelist who's writing a story on the Cardinals' pitchers for *Vanity Fair*. Occasionally it takes a person with totally fresh perspective—someone from out-

coach, Hub Kittle, never shows the pitchers what they're doing wrong. He shows them pictures of when they're going well to remind them of the right way to do things."

The reason players are spoiled isn't so much because they're well paid but because they're pampered. Cardinal players have everything taken care of—laundry, travel, even golf reservations at private courses on off-days. The club picks up hotel bills, and players take care of meals (the postgame clubhouse spread is free) and other incidentals out of their $43.50 per diem. We took an Ozark charter tonight from Cincinnati to Houston, and it was first-class all the way. The team bus carried us from the ball park directly to the spot on the airport ramp where our plane was waiting. There was so much room on board that everyone who wanted an empty seat next to him had one. Food? We started off with a cold appetizer featuring shrimp, lobster, artichoke and lox. Then it was on to a main course of either lobster, chicken or Chateaubriand. There was a spinach salad, and the flight attendants offered assorted cakes and pastries for dessert. I had a rum ball and topped it off with amaretto in a chocolate cup.

Pitcher Joaquin Andujar had been grousing about something or other during the bus ride to the plane. During the flight outfielder George Hendrick ragged him mercilessly. After landing, we piled into a waiting bus. The order of seating was roughly the same as it had been on the plane—coaches and managers up front, followed by writers, then players. Arriving at Houston's Shamrock Hilton Hotel, the players took their pre-assigned room keys and headed upstairs. Their luggage would be brought up to them. By now Andujar was smiling and joking. He had nothing to complain about. Neither did his teammates.

MAY 28 — "Where else but in a bleeping kids' game can you start at night and end up in the morning?" Cardinal coach Red Schoendienst called out at 12:10 a.m. "God a'mighty, ain't it wonderful!"

We'd just seen an extraordinary, 18-inning game that the Cardinals had won 3–1. In the last of the 17th the Astros had had a man on third with one out when Alan Ashby had hit a ball deep in the hole. Everyone had assumed the game was over. Either the ball would go through, scoring a run, or shortstop Ozzie Smith would field it too late to throw home. But Smith had dived, grabbed the ball and leaped to his feet in one motion. Then he'd checked the runner back to third and thrown out Ashby by two steps. He'd also thrown out the next runner. The Cardinals had rallied to win the game in the 18th.

"Best shortstop in the history of the game!" croaked Kittle, who has been in baseball 48 years. The rest of us walked around the clubhouse with great big smiles on our faces. "I'd pay to watch Ozzie Smith," I kept saying.

Then something struck me: Scenes like this don't occur very often these days. I don't want to romanticize the lot of old-time ballplayers, who had lousy salaries, poor medical care and virtually no rights, but they may have enjoyed the game more than today's major-leaguers. Baseball was their reason for living, and they loved playing. Today's players think constantly about money: How much they make, how much others make, how little time they may have to strike it rich. No one wants to turn the clock back, but I wish there were more pure, joyous scenes like the one in the Cardinals' clubhouse. We're forever talking moneyball, not baseball.

JUNE 1—With the Angels in New York, where I live, I called up my closest friend on the team, third baseman Doug DeCinces. He couldn't meet me for lunch, but he did offer an alternative—sitting with his wife, Kristi, at the ballpark.

The visiting wives' seats are along the third-base line at Yankee Stadium, and we sat just a couple of rows from the field. This vantage point presented an interesting look at the world

of a player's wife. The DeCinceses have two children, Timmy, 9, and Amy, 3, and Kristi hopes that Doug, who's 32, retires soon enough to spend more time with the kids. "But not too soon," she said sensibly. "He hasn't done everything he'd like to do in baseball, and he has to get it out of his system." Nevertheless, the time apart isn't easy for either of them, and Doug's constantly sore back has both of them worried. "I pray for him a lot," Kristi said.

After the game we had dinner at the Century Restaurant in midtown Manhattan. As is often the case, our conversation was as much personal as it was professional. Doug said he doesn't get on umpires much anymore. "I know that they're doing what they want to do, that no one's forcing them to, but it's still a thankless job. They never get noticed until they blow one." Asked why managers are constantly arguing with umpires, he said, "It's partly to show the players they're behind them, but also to take the heat off the players. The manager wants to get between the player and the umpire before the player starts screaming and gets thrown out."

JUNE 14—The Cardinals and Phillies played an excellent game tonight in St. Louis, but the highlight of my day was a postgame drink I had with Joe Morgan, the Phillies' second baseman. Morgan is one of the brightest people in the game.

He told me he's living in a Philadelphia apartment while his wife and two daughters remain on the West Coast. He misses them, but he doesn't want to disrupt their lives. "My wife runs a women's clothing store," Morgan said. "She's known as Gloria Morgan, not Mrs. Joe Morgan. I think that's great. I hope it rubs off on the girls."

Morgan once wanted to manage. No more, he said. "There are too many guys who don't know the fundamentals. They think all they have to do is show up at three or four o'clock. I could never manage because I see so many things that bother me. Suppose there's a runner on first. The first baseman has to keep him close, and that creates a huge gap on the right side of the infield. So you'd think they'd do everything possible to keep the batter from hitting over there. But they don't. They're pitching inside to left-handed batters!"

Morgan was right. Because of expansion, more and more players are being brought up who aren't sufficiently schooled in fundamentals and strategy. And long-term contracts don't reward the guy who can move up the runner. "I'm not opposed to big salaries, but I wish they'd tie them to team play," Morgan said.

JULY 6—I felt both pleasure and disappointment—pleasure at attending the festivities surrounding the 50th Anniversary All-Star Game, disappointment at having missed so many of these occasions in the past. The White Sox, who hosted the first game in 1933, have put on a gala golden anniversary celebration. At yesterday's Old Timers Game, stars old and new mingled in the clubhouse.

"Is this your locker?" Willie Mays asked Andre Dawson.

"No, sir, it's yours," said Dawson.

Following the Old Timers Game, the White Sox threw a party at Navy Pier. The central figure there was Ron Kittle of the White Sox, who has become the most popular athlete in town. Kittle stood in the ballroom wearing snake-skin boots, slacks, an open shirt and a sports jacket. "I'm not wearing my glasses," he said. "I don't want to be recognized."

What a joke. Everyone was after Kittie's autograph—little kids, old men and women of all descriptions, including the wives of other ballplayers. In Chicago, a city of few sports heroes and even fewer winning teams, Kittle is already a bigger hero than Mr. Cub, Ernie Banks, ever was. Banks says so himself.

After the Old Timers Game, Kittle grabbed a bat and ran around the American League club

sensitive man, he's driven to distraction by the demands of auto-graph seekers. "They were calling me at seven, nine in the morning in Chicago," he said. Carew wearily girded for the next assault. Assuming an extreme Boston accent, he called out, "Gimme da bawl, sign heeyah."

JULY 8—DeCinces is suffering from a rib separation and has aggravated the injury by trying to come back too soon. I pointed out to him that The Baseball Encyclopedia is filled with the names of men who ruined their careers by playing with injuries. "No question," Doug said. "You're under a lot of pressure—from your peers, from the writers asking you every day how you feel, from the fans and, most of all, from yourself. You want to keep your stats up, and you know your team needs you in the lineup. I'm having a good year, and any time I don't play, a lefthanded pitcher who faces us is going to benefit."

Nonetheless, I hope Doug doesn't play during the three-game series in Boston. The back injury has led to spasms, and he feels great pain every time he throws or stretches for a grounder. I breathed a deep sigh of relief when he wasn't used in the All-Star Game, except to pinch-hit. Today he went out to the park four hours before game time, took a heat massage, used an electronic muscle-stimulator to move fresh blood into the damaged area and lifted some weights. An hour or so later Arthur Pappas, the Red Sox physician, poked Doug's ribs. He immediately went into a back spasm. "No way you're playing today," Pappas said.

JULY 9—I overheard the California trainer say that Doug was considering traction. A few minutes later I found Doug in the clubhouse. He was distraught. "I thought I could DH today, but I can't even run," he said. "The problem is, the rib condition keeps affecting my back. Maybe I should go into traction, take some drugs and do nothing for a while. Or maybe I'll have to give up the month of July. But then I think of the numbers I need to have this year."

I tried to put myself in his position. He's making about $400,000 a year and will become a free agent at season's end, the Angels having refused to negotiate a contract extension with him last spring. On the open market he'll be worth $1 million a year, the going rate for premium third basemen. But now, with his medical condition, it could all go poof: the contract, the career, the future. At least, that's what has to be going through his mind. No wonder he's depressed.

[Fortunately, DeCinces rested long enough to recover. After playing regularly and well in August and September, he signed a three-year, $3 million contract with the Angels.]

JULY 13—The Reds' incomparable catcher, Johnny Bench, is retiring after this season, and as he makes his final appearance in each National League city, he's receiving a fond farewell. Today at Shea Stadium he's getting a send-off from New York fans and players.

Mets pitcher Tom Seaver: "John was never intimidated by the tag play at the plate, no matter what the collision was going to be like. He and Jerry Grote were two of the best I've ever seen at blocking home, throwing out runners and giving the umpire a good view of the ball as it came over the plate."

Mets broadcaster Tim McCarver, a former catcher: "Bench was the best one-handed catcher ever. In fact, he popularized using one hand. Before about 1940, Birdie Tebbetts and others said to catch with two hands. That's a bunch of bananas. When you catch one-handed, you can snap the ball right back to your throwing hand, whereas the movement's too bulky with two hands. With one, it's an oval-like movement.

"The other thing John popularized was the hinged glove, as opposed to the old ones with the little pocket in the middle. If you caught everything in the pocket, it would sting your hand,

some hits. The things I hated most were the foul tips. But when I was a world champion, all the aches and pains went away.

"I had the ability to change the game with the one-handed glove. I could stand away from a sliding runner and avoid a collision by making a sweeping tag. You just have to go '¡Olé!' like a guy making the tag at second. Catchers never had the time to do that when they had to use two hands with the round glove. You've got to keep the ball moving to make the sweep tag; don't just put the glove in front of the runner's foot. It's like catching an egg: You've got to give with it.

"Handling pitchers? There were different personalities. There was the guy you patted on the back, the guy you had to tell about different situations and the guy you just told, 'Let's go.' If a pitcher believes in you, he'll throw his best pitch. I may get away from a pitch when he's not throwing it well, and then come back to it later. You spot it."

Easy As Three To One

(*Originally published in* Sports Illustrated. *1979 Time Inc.*
Reprinted with permission of Sports Illustrated.)

To the public, spring training is as immutable as a Norman Rockwell cover: swaying palm trees; players leaning over the grandstand fence, chatting with elderly spectators; groups of pitchers jogging on the outfield warning track; pepper games.

To players, spring training is more complex and specialized. There are, for example, the arcane devices used in March and rarely, if ever, after: bazooka guns for pop-ups; fully enclosed wire-mesh batting cages; sand pits for sliding; pitching machines. The players also spend hours working on the game's intricacies, which they will practice only briefly, if at all, come April. In fact, some of these plays or their variations rarely occur during the season. But when they do, the players must instantaneously recall the lessons of spring and react instinctively. Bunting, now down the first-base line, now toward third, is the subject of lengthy drills. So are pickoffs, double-play tosses, relays, cutoffs and calling for pop-ups (always either "I got it" or "*Lo tengo*").

An onlooker might well wonder why some of the drills are conducted at all. How often does one see a pickoff play at third? All the time in spring training. And one wonders why some drills aren't undertaken more frequently. The play that most often seems to be messed up in games is the rundown. There are invariably too many fielders involved, too many throws and too many mistakes. "When it gets practiced in the spring, you see all kinds of instructors," says one veteran. "There's mass confusion. They should simplify it."

By contrast, a tricky spring-training drill that's generally well executed in the summer is that tantalizing race to the bag—grounder to first, pitcher covering. This is as it should be, because that play is the very symbol of spring training.

"It's a gathering time, like a class reunion," says Jim Kaat of the Phillies, one of baseball's best-fielding pitchers. "All of a sudden you're in the home room, with 19 or 20 pitchers standing around talking about what happened during the winter." It's also a doubly useful drill, as the Cardinals' Keith Hernandez, the National League's Gold Glove first baseman in 1978, observes. "It satisfies everyone. The pitchers get their running and fielding, and the first basemen get their grounders."

The drill takes longer than any other because of the number of players involved. All the pitchers—veterans, rookies, minor-leaguers up for a quick look—participate, along with three or four first basemen. A weathered coach bats out the grounders that set the play in motion.

it's because the pitcher didn't get a jump." Kaat heads for a spot 10 to 15 feet down the line from the base. Then he turns sharply left and races parallel to the line, toward the base. If all goes well, he catches the first baseman's toss a couple of steps ahead of the base. Then he looks for first and touches it with his right foot to avoid colliding with the runner. "If you practice it enough," says Kaat, "you'll get your footwork down like a hurdler."

Of course, the play is not as simple as the neat 3–1 on your scorecard. For one thing, the throw doesn't always go from first baseman to pitcher. A bunt or a slowly topped grounder can be fielded by either player. If both go for the ball, the second baseman should cover first. But for some reason, he rarely participates in the spring-training drill.

Hernandez feels that first basemen make more mistakes on the play than pitchers. "Usually it's the throw—ahead, behind, low or high," he says. A good fielding pitcher, such as Phil Niekro of the Braves, never anticipates an accurate throw. "I look for the bad ones, because I know I can handle the good ones," he says. Niekro also doesn't panic about tagging first. Pitchers usually err when they look for the base before they have the ball.

The play looks simple enough when the ball is hit sharply and directly at the first baseman, who then flips an underhand throw, chest-high, to the pitcher a couple of steps before he reaches the bag. Things start getting complicated, both in practice and in games, when the ball is hit any distance to the first baseman's

right. An underhand toss won't get the job done in such instanc-
es; the throw must then be sidearm or overhand. This situation
is one of the few in which a right-handed first baseman has an
advantage over a left-hander. True, the right-hander must backhand the grounder, but after that all he has to do is straighten up
and throw. The left-hander must field the ball and turn clockwise,
back to the plate, before making his toss. "You're deep in the hole
and you're probably off-balance," says Hernandez. "The pitcher's
going full speed and you have to lead him just right."

To a perfectionist the solution seems simple — take the drill
north. "Why not?" asks Niekro. "Most teams run the drill only
as punishment, but it should be part of the season. It's one of the
fundamentals of baseball."

JULY 28 — I'm observing the pine-tar episode from afar—vaca-
tioning on Martha's Vineyard—but I didn't have to be at Yankee
Stadium to understand its significance. I have no doubt it will be
the highlight of the season. Why? Because it's something we can
all get our hooks into. It's funny, serious; complicated, simple;
trivial, important. It's baseball at its best, with new angles and
controversies sure to open up every day. People will argue about
it for weeks.

[The Cardozo Law Review will run two or three articles
about the pine-tar incident in its issue that comes out in March.
The pieces will touch on many basic legal subjects including free
speech; rules interpretation; the spirit vs. the letter of the law;
commercial law; sports and the law; the appellate system; and
statutory vs. common law. My father, Benjamin, a retired member
of the Massachusetts Supreme Court and an emeritus professor of
law at Harvard, says: "For anyone interested in a legal career, this
could be the place to start."]

AUG. 3 — Today Bowie Kuhn abdicated as commissioner, and the
owners began referring to him as though he were some kind of
god. My own feelings are considerably more mixed. I'll say this
for Bowie: He stood up to some very difficult owners, and his veto
of the Charlie Finley player sales in 1976 was a noble gesture.
Unlike many baseball executives, Kuhn undoubtedly lay awake at
night wondering what was in the best interest of the game. But I

feel he too frequently came to the wrong conclusion, supporting as he did the designated-hitter rule, nighttime playoffs and Series games and every manner of commercial scheme to promote baseball: a relief award named after an antacid, a playoff award given by a car company, a Series sweepstakes sponsored by a cookie company. Under Kuhn baseball ceased being a pastime and became a product.

of subjects.

Are today's ballplayers better prepared for life after baseball than previous generations? "With long-term contracts, you have time to think about the future," Curtis said. "Before, you played a year at a time. Suddenly, you were out of baseball, wondering what you'd do next."

How tough is it to stay in shape from year to year? "When I was young," said Curtis, now 35, "I'd relax all winter and get in shape for spring training. Now I have to keep in shape all year." I asked him to name the best manager he ever played for. "Joe Altobelli," he said unhesitatingly, citing the man's thoughtfulness and consideration.

"Baseball's something that you pass through," he concluded. "I have to keep telling myself that how I play has nothing to do with what kind of person I am. Sometimes I find myself saying, 'I just gave up seven runs—am I that bad a guy?' You can't take it personally."

OCT. 5—Allow me an instant between the white lines, if only to explain something that occurs outside them. To qualify as a great play, something must occur at a critical juncture in an important game. How many heroic achievements have passed unnoticed because they didn't affect the outcome?

It can even occur in a playoff. Tonight, Morgan had one of the finest innings in the history of second base. It attracted little notice because it didn't determine the result. With the game tied 1–1 in the fourth and L.A.'s Ken Landreaux on first, Mike Marshall hit a hard grounder up the middle. Morgan ran it down and forced the speedy Landreaux by diving and tagging second with the ball. "It was the only play I had," Morgan said later.

Bill Russell then singled Marshall to third, and on the first pitch to Jack Fimple, Russell took off for second. Catcher Bo Diaz threw to Morgan in plenty of time, but Russell deliberately stopped midway between the bags.

Now Morgan was in a position second basemen dread. "This is the way the play works," he explained. "I come over to take the throw from the catcher. If the base stealer continues running, I tag him. Otherwise, my job is to run him down without letting the runner score."

Like a vaudeville dancer crossing the stage, Morgan ran toward first with his head cocked toward the third-base line. Marshall made a few feints and charged home. By waiting to throw to Diaz until the right moment, Morgan set up the rundown that got Marshall out.

Ah, but Russell had taken second on the play. And when Fimple sent a liner toward right-center, the Dodgers had surely taken the lead. But Morgan leaped high to spear the ball and end the inning. It was an extraordinary performance, too good to be forgotten even though the Phillies lost 4–1.

OCT. 13 — The World Series isn't an especially pleasant event for sportswriters. For one thing, there are so many of us that it's almost impossible to get a player alone. For another, most games are played on cold October nights. And the Series has lost some of its importance because of the playoffs. That's where the real pressure is. After surviving those tense, three-of-five championship series, players are happy just to be in the World Series. Getting there is the goal; winning the Series has become secondary.

What makes the Series worthwhile is the spectacle. At tonight's World Series party the Phillies set out a cake shaped like

Veterans Stadium; waitresses wore period-piece costumes; there were Philadelphia-style cheesesteak sandwiches and retired greats were all around. I shook hands with Vic Power, perhaps the best-fielding righthanded first baseman in history (for my money, the Mets' Keith Hernandez is the best lefty).

And the talk isn't half bad at the Series, either. I got into a con-

Right. And nothing against Rod Carew, who'll make the Hall with all those batting titles, but as a clutch hitter he couldn't hold a candle to Killebrew," said Kaat. [In his fourth year on the ballot, Killebrew finally made the Hall this January. Maybe there's hope for Kaat.]

"[Pittsburgh manager] Chuck Tanner saved my career in 1974 when we were both with the White Sox," Kaat continued. "I'd started out at 4–1. Then I lost six straight and everyone was getting on me. I felt awful. Tanner called me into his office and said there was nothing wrong with the way I was throwing, that he'd put me in the bullpen a week and then start me again. I wound up 21–13 and won 20 the next year."

I asked Kaat if there's anything to the sophomore jinx. He said there is. "When you're a rookie, no one expects anything of you. If you've had a good season, though, you start setting goals for the next year and people watch you more carefully. The pressure is really on."

Before being released by the Cardinals this summer, Kaat had become close friends with reliever Bruce Sutter. The word around the league late in the season was that Sutter had lost his stuff. "I don't think so," said Kaat. "The problem was, there were long periods when he didn't get to pitch because there were no save situations. He lost his rhythm, not his stuff. Of course, that can happen to any pitcher early in the season, when there are so many days

off and rainouts. One possibility would be to use three pitchers a game, each for three innings. But managers won't do that because what will people say if they take out a guy who's going well and the next pitcher gets bombed? The manager won't look good, so he won't do it. So much of baseball is covering yourself."

OCT. 31—My baseball odyssey could only end at the Hall of Fame in Cooperstown, N.Y. Upon arriving today, I went right downstairs to the Hall of Fame gallery housing the 184 brass plaques, one for each inductee. At one end of the rectangular room is the Hall of Fame Trophy for the winner of the annual major league exhibition game played in Cooperstown, and at the other a striking obelisk honoring the ballplayers who served in the armed forces. Lining the sides are tall marble columns. And set back in alcoves behind the columns are the plaques.

I found myself reading every word on each plaque, and I noticed that the tone of the wording doesn't change from one era's immortals to the next. Grover Cleveland Alexander struck out Tony Lazzeri with the bases loaded in the final "crisis" of the 1926 World Series. Henry Aaron led all baseball in "long [extra-base] hits." "I've tried to keep the same style," said the Hall's publicity director, Bill Guilfoile, who has been writing the inscriptions for the past few years. "The only change I've been making is to cut down on the wordage, because some of the plaques seemed so crowded." Guilfoile should make an addition, though, on a plaque he inherited. The one honoring Jackie Robinson doesn't mention that he integrated baseball. But Branch Rickey's plaque says he brought Robinson to the majors. [I learned years later that Robinson wanted his plaque to detail only his baseball accomplishments. He wanted to be known as a Hall of Fame player beyond his extraordinary contribution to the game and a more just America. Today, at his family's insistence, the plaque now refers to his integrating the majors.]

I had few objections to other exhibits. My passion for defense was whetted when I looked at old mitts, some as small as golf gloves. No wonder Harry Hooper, a major-leaguer from 1909 to

1925 and one of the best right-fielders ever, had a career fielding percentage of only .966.

But what permeates the Hall is the aura of the Babe. The Babe photographed at his induction ceremony—tieless, socks falling around his ankles. The Babe, smiling, pictured with his two favorite companions—kids and women. The Babe in old film footage,

felt. Here was the best of baseball, frozen in time and space. The owners and entrepreneurs can tinker with rules and rituals—but not with history.

CHAPTER SEVEN

It's How He Calls The Game

Tim McCarver Was Once Best-Known As Catcher to Carlton. Now He's Gained Real Fame As Voice of the Mets.

(Previously published in the Philadelphia Inquirer Magazine *on September 21, 1986. Used with permission of Philadelphia Inquirer, Copyright 2016. All rights reserved.)*

It had already been a busy day for Tim McCarver. Rising at 8:30. Taping radio sports monologues from 10:30 to 1. Setting up interviews with four TV critics. Lunch, a quick nap. Now he was ready to meet his colleague Steve Zabriskie and drive to Shea Stadium for the main order of business: broadcasting the New York Mets. But no, the phone rang, and a reporter on deadline had to ask some questions. And lo, the rarest of things—Tim McCarver 10 minutes behind schedule.

'I hate to be late," he said, leaving the Manhattan hotel he occupies during the season. "And I don't much like people who are late."

It's all McCarver can do to keep up with himself these days. A half dozen years ago, he completed his baseball playing career, exiting respectably as the personal catcher for Philadelphia pitcher Steve Carlton, then segueing neatly into the Phillies broadcast booth. Three years later he went to work for the Mets. Now he's arguably the hottest name in baseball television—a cult figure among Mets fans, a fixture on national ABC games of the week, an honored voice on All-Star and post-season broadcasts.

"He turned on the city even before the Mets started winning," says Stan Isaacs, the noted sports TV critic for Newsday. "He's engaging and sharp, he cares about words, and he adds color, personality, and richness of anecdote."

McCarver arrived at the garage around the corner from his hotel and ordered the Buick the Mets have leased for him ("One of the perks of the job," he said, almost apologetically). With his snub nose and crooked smile and twinkling eyes, he's elfin Irish

ing now, the earlier lateness forgotten. The ballpark beckoned, where something exciting happens every day—or where Tim McCarver makes something exciting happen. He would even make a happening of the ride there.

McCarver, 44, is as convivial as a game-show host and as cordial as a caterer, but he's no phony or lightweight. Artifice and pretense annoy him. If you want him to like you, don't say, "Have a nice day." Never call him on the phone without immediately identifying yourself. Always make eye contact and listen carefully—just as he does to you. And expect to be challenged if you make a superficial observation. Indeed, without being asked, McCarver was now mocking the twin devils of his 1986 season—two familiar and increasingly irksome questions:

(1) Will the Mets become complacent with their big lead over the National League's East Division? "If there's anything a ballplayer or manager hates, it's complacency," McCarver said. "Words like complacency and pressure aren't in their vocabulary." As McCarver knows, a big lead is one of the most energy-giving phenomena in sports. Every day, the team finds a new way to win. The players can't wait to go to the park.

(2) What's wrong with Dwight Gooden? The Cy Young Award winner as the NL's best pitcher when he went 24–4 in 1985, Gooden was 10–4 on this mid-July day but just 5–4 over the last two months. "Every time I go downtown, people ask me

that. The problem is that people keep comparing him to what he did last year. He may never be that good again. There are too many things involved for people to know what's wrong. He might stride too far, causing him to push the ball. He's been wild early in the count. Batters have been laying off the high fastball they'd been chasing out of the strike zone. It's a lot of little things, adding up to a mild problem. But people keep asking."

Did he have other pet peeves about baseball? "Let me count the ways," he began. "Ballplayers wearing jackets to contain the body heat when it's 90 degrees out. For that matter, riding to a game with a bunch of pitchers who tell you to turn off the air conditioner because air will get on their arms. The righty-lefty business," he said of the managerial practice of bringing in a righthanded pitcher to face a righthanded batter or a lefty pitcher to face one or two southpaw swingers; also, using righthanded batters against lefthanded pitchers and lefthanded batters against righthanded pitchers. "This is changing because people are asking questions. Tons of righthanded batters hit righthanded pitchers better than lefthanders; I prefer a lefthanded pitcher who can get more than one or two batters out. People cling to tradition without thinking. It's stupid."

McCarver was in form—provocative, engaging, enlightening. Looking amused, he admired a pedestrian crossing the street like a broken-field runner. "New York is an angling town," he said, "as opposed to an Anglican town."

Now we were getting vintage Tim McCarver. We're talking nonstop punster here. McCarver drops puns on all occasions: in his sleep, at the breakfast table, in the car, on the air. Lenny Dykstra, a Mets outfielder whose hat jars loose when he's chasing fly balls, belongs to the fraternity Kappa Sku. Pedro Guerrero, the Dodger leftfielder who suffered a knee injury this spring and was operated on by the famed cutter Frank Jobe, was, McCarver once remarked, "one of the patients of Jobe."

Picking a token out of the ashtray at the Triborough Bridge, McCarver began speaking about his profession. "I don't like to screw up on the air," he said, "but I do like to have fun. It's a fine line. My motto is: Prepare, relax, let it fly. Enjoy the game. Don't act natural. Be natural."

That statement shields the seriousness of purpose behind Mc-Carver's style. "'I've been broadcasting 20 years, and I've never heard anyone as informative or entertaining," says Zabriskie. "He's worked very hard to improve himself. I've learned a lot about baseball from him, and I hope he's learned a lot about announcing from me."

one else on the field can claim that. Also, we're always looking for little things like shoulders and front feet, so it's easy to point out what other people miss."

For instance, in this year's All-Star Game, Cubs second baseman Ryne Sandberg ran to his right to knock down a grounder; the batter was safe on what looked like would be ruled a sure hit. Not to McCarver. "What an infielder tries to do when he backhands a ball...(is) catch the ball in the webbing. And that ball hit the heel of the glove of Sandberg. He actually went too far." The official scorer agreed and gave Sandberg an error.

"I'm very careful to call the Mets 'they,'" says McCarver. "I've never overlooked how difficult the game is, but I think the struggle is worth talking about. If a manager struggles, he's better. If you struggle, you may be better able to put words together, because you look for reasons. When I talk about a catcher's throwing problems, I know. Anyway, when you've been critical of a player, the praise you give him has more validity."

But McCarver is not the kind of announcer who stirs up artificial controversies. As a former signal-caller, he's particularly sensitive about second-guessing strategy. So he usually first-guesses. Earlier this season he noted that Dykstra was playing the field "in another area code." Sure enough, a line drive that he would have caught if he'd been correctly positioned fell in front of him. When McCarver criticizes a play past, he speaks like a teacher correcting a faulty essay. Shortstop Rafael Santana started a would-be double play too quickly. Why? Because it was more important at that stage of the game to get a sure out at second than to risk an error on a muff or hurried throw. Darryl Strawberry did well to tag at first and bluff running to second on a fly ball; he'd have done better to continue there after the outfielder delayed his throw.

McCarver thrives on "inside baseball." He'll explain why a righthanded batter takes longer running to first when jammed by a pitch than when thrown away (an inside pitch drives him to third, an outside one leads him toward first). These observations come thick and fast. If there's one accomplishment above all others that McCarver should be noted for, it's analysis. He has proved that fans want more than glitz, cheering and drug talk. In the wake of his success, announcers everywhere can no longer patronize their viewers; they must dissect a baseball game like a doctor doing an autopsy.

The car pulled up at Shea, and McCarver walked a gantlet of well-wishers to copy down the lineups in the Met offices. "Chance favors a prepared man," he said, quoting Douglas MacArthur.

McCarver carries notebooks with information on every player in each league. On Fernando Valenzuela: "Walks have progressed in 4 yrs. (guys laying off screwball)." A lot of the information comes from the teams' press guides, McCarver concedes, but some detail might remind him to ask a question. Before the game, he reviews stats and facts, skipping dinner to remain as sharp as the players. But above all else, he hangs out at the batting cage and in the clubhouse. "So much of the game is absorption," he explained. "You want nuance. You want to understand. The one question you want to keep asking is, 'Why?'"

"Most reporters ask psychological questions," said Mets third baseman Ray Knight. "They'll want to know, 'Do you have momentum, are you under added pressure?' Tim will ask why the Pirates let Sid Bream hit away with men on first and second and one out."

McCarver knew just what to ask the Braves' Bob Horner when they met during batting practice. Horner had recently tied a major-league record with four homers in one game, and McCarver wanted to know what he was thinking before he hit the fourth one in the ninth inning. "We were down four runs with two outs, and Reardon (Montreal pitcher Jeff Reardon) was the pitcher," Horner said. "I was just looking for a fastball to hit."

As usual, McCarver had a story at hand. "You were only the 11th player to do it, and the second on a team that lost the game.

the clubhouse saying, "Ozzie Virgil, call your sister." The sign referred to Ozzie Jr.'s father, a former San Diego coach. "You had to wonder why his sister didn't know he'd been released and signed with Seattle," McCarver said, "so I got on the air and said, 'Ozzie Virgil, Call Your Sister.' The other night, there were banners saying 'Ozzie Virgil Jr., Call Your Aunt.' Now there are people in T-shirts telling me to call my sister. It's unbelievable.'" Indeed, that very night there would be 'Ozzie Virgil, Please Pay Your Phone Bill' and 'Tim McCarver, Please Call My Sister.' There's only one word for such a continuing gag, and McCarver knows it: "Lettermanesque."

McCarver entered the broadcast booth looking for more fun. Someone handed him an announcement about the birthday of a Mets employee that he was to read on the air. McCarver chuckled and began reading to Zabriskie: "Year after year, he does an excellent job for the Mets, great guy, terrific golfer, and to know him is to love him."

"To love him!" Zabriskie roared. "They even wrote him a script!"

"A scripted happy birthday!" said McCarver. "I do like the guy, but give me a rest." (He later made the announcement in considerably more subdued language.)

McCarver produced a Robert Francis poem, "The Pitcher," that a fan had sent in. "I love this," he said, reading the entire text aloud.

His art is eccentricity, his aim
How not to hit the mark he seems to aim at,
His passion how to avoid the obvious,
His techniques how to vary the avoidance.
The others throw to be comprehended. He
Throws to be a moment misunderstood.
Yet not too much. Not errant, arrant, wild,
But every seeming aberration willed.
Not to, yet still, still to communicate
Making the batter understand too late.

"'Vary the avoidance'—I like that," said McCarver. "We might be able to work this in if Ojeda (Mets lefthander Bob Ojeda) has a good game. He's probably the best pure pitcher on the staff, and the poem could describe him well."

McCarver broadcasts 90 games a year for commercial WOR-TV with Ralph Kiner and Zabriskie, and 60 a year for the cable SportsChannel with Kiner and Fran Healy. The men alternate play-by-play and color duties, two partners on the air together for three innings at a time. The idea is to have two guys conversing pleasantly, like fans in the stands.

There's no question which segment the viewers like best: the three innings with McCarver and Kiner. They look perfect together, sitting in their shirtsleeves and club ties, smoking hand-wrapped Honduran cigars, leaning forward at the same angle, kidding and laughing, McCarver's voice rising at the end of sentences, Kiner deadpanning.

Kiner, a Hall-of-Fame slugger for the Pirates and Cubs, has been a Mets broadcaster since the club's inception in 1962. He's been with them through thick and thin—his own as an announcer as well as the club's as a team—and the universal feeling is that McCarver has rekindled his spirit.

"Bob and Ray may not have been good as individuals," Kiner, 63, says of the comedians, "but they were great as a team. Timmy makes broadcasting a lot more fun. He has that enthusiasm and quick wit and soie de vivre." Kiner means joie de vivre. He is long

remembered for his malaprops, little noted for his superb knowledge of baseball history, trivia and anecdote. "History's a big part
of this game, the charm of it," Kiner says. "The game's basically
the same, except for the designated hitter. When I say a guy hit
.330 in 1916, the viewer can relate it to 1980. And Timmy can
relate everything to the facts of modern life. We bounce back and

shots with their insights. The three men jibe like peanut butter
and jelly on white bread.

This time the interplay was almost subliminal. Early in the
broadcast, Webb flashed to an Atlanta coach in headphones. Mc-
Carver explained that the man was conversing with the "eye in
the sky"—a Braves employee situated at press level to reposition
the fielders. Webb showed a blimp outside the park. "'That's not
the eye in the sky," said Kiner.

The bottom of the second inning opened with a visual of a triple play the Cubs had pulled off in a recent game. "And coming in
now...a man who never hit into a triple play—Tim McCarver,"
Kiner said.

McCarver: "I was involved in one as a baserunner....I was
just told to watch the line drive, and I didn't."

Kiner: "In 1962 the Mets ended their season when Joe Pignatano hit into a triple play....As they walked off the field, Casey
Stengel said, 'Don't worry about it, it was a team effort.'"

A few minutes later McCarver mentioned that Chuck Tanner,
the Braves' Panglossian manager, would be Kiner's guest on his
postgame show. "I guess that upsets our producer-director Bill
Webb," McCarver said.

"He's the antithesis of Chuck Tanner," said Kiner. "Got a very
even disposition—always mad."

Webb showed a cloud of smoke in the distance.

But mainly there was McCarver's quick wit and insight, and Kiner's historical perspective. Atlanta pitcher Zane Smith reminded Kiner of author Zane Grey, a former minor-league player. McCarver and Kiner agreed that Mets centerfielder Mookie Wilson misjudged a ball before making a shoestring catch. The viewer could see what had happened; McCarver knew why. "Mookie misjudged the ball because, as the Platters used to say, heavenly shades of night are falling, it's twilight time."

In one of his last observations before taking off innings four through six, McCarver gave the viewers something to remember him by. Zane Smith was "going too much to the breaking ball," he said, first-guessing disaster if changes weren't made. Then McCarver took a break for the first time since he'd arrived at the park.

James Timothy McCarver obviously was born with an independent streak. His great-great-grandfather, an immigrant from Ireland, gave up cranberry farming in Minnesota to move to Memphis and fight for the Confederacy. But when Tim and his friends played corkball, a stickball hybrid featuring weighted corks and broomsticks, Tim would create fantasy broadcasts and identify himself as Monte Irvin, the black Hall of Famer.

This was nothing special for a family in which a future big-leaguer's first coach was his big sister. "Marilyn's seven years older than I am," says McCarver, the fourth of five children. "She used to roll balls for me to hit—I guess that's how I became a low-ball hitter. She also had the novel idea for me to bat lefthanded. She'd been following the game from the time she was 7 or 8, and she figured I'd have an edge with those steps to first you get batting lefthanded."

The tough son of a Memphis cop, McCarver attended Christian Brothers, an all-male Catholic high school. "The brothers would waylay you in a minute—whack you—and that was exactly what I needed," says McCarver. "They were also great teachers. I especially remember my 12th-grade English teacher, Brother William, who gave me an appreciation of the language. He'd bring the Macbeth records into class. "McCarver is probably the only ex-jock ever to say, "As Lady Macbeth said, what's done cannot be undone."

McCarver played four sports—baseball, football, track and basketball—and was offered a football scholarship to Notre Dame for his two-way end play. But baseball's St. Louis Cardinals seduced him with a big-money offer for those pre-free-agent days: a $75,000 signing bonus and $30,000 in salary, paid out at $21,000 a year for five seasons. McCarver wasted no time in jus-

forerunner of today's mobile catchers, he once led the National League in triples. "I hated to see him up with men on base because he always came through," says Cincinnati first baseman Tony Perez. "There was no way to pitch him because he hit the ball all over the place."

A natural leader, McCarver kept clubhouses loose with his Frank Fontaine imitations and had kind words for teammates after good games and bad alike ("Affirmation is very important"). He also had a knack for criticizing a player's performance without incurring resentment. Over a 162-game season, these intangible qualities contribute as much to winning baseball as strikeout pitchers and home-run hitters. McCarver played on three pennant winners in St. Louis and one pennant and three division winners in Philadelphia and had a cup of coffee with the Red Sox while they were winning the American League championship in 1975. "I don't rate players," says Cincinnati player-manager Pete Rose, "but his teams won."

As a player, McCarver is best remembered for top-notch catching, his average arm notwithstanding. He was catching for St. Louis in 1968 when Bob Gibson had the best season in modern pitching history—a 22–9 record and an otherworldly 1.12 earned run average. With the Cardinals in the 1960s and Philadelphia in the 1970s, McCarver handled 300-game winner Carlton and eventually became Silent Steve's pipeline to the world. McCarver jokes that pitchers ordered him off the mound and threw their own games. McCarver-watchers know better.

"He was sensitive to a pitcher's needs," says Jim Kaat, a 283-game winner now broadcasting for the Yankees. "In 1978 I was on the verge of being released by the Phillies. I had what looked like one more start. Tim took me aside, and we prepared as if it were the last game of the World Series. I'd been in the American League, where you can get lefthanded batters out by pitching them outside. He reminded me that, possibly because they'd been taught to slap outside pitches on artificial turf, lefthanders in the National League are better worked inside. I went six innings and struck out something like nine batters. They couldn't release me." Kaat's career lasted another six seasons.

"Tim knew what sequences to call the pitches in, and he made the game go faster," says Mets manager Davey Johnson, a former teammate and opponent. "I used to love arguing with him because he's so adamant. That's a good way for a catcher to be."

"Sometimes just slapping down those pitches with authority is a big plus," McCarver says of signaling the pitcher which pitch to throw. "A tentative signal makes for a tentative pitch. A confident signal can make for a confident pitch, which may be successful even if it wasn't the textbook pitch you should have called. You also want to call your pitches briskly to establish a rhythm with your pitcher. The knock on Carlton Fisk"—the Red Sox and White Sox catcher who works like a monk over a manuscript—"was that he was too deliberate. As Jim Kaat used to say, if you work long, you work wrong."

McCarver seemed to work just right. The first time he met Carlton was in the spring of 1965. Carlton was a rookie, McCarver an established star. In his first spring outing, Carlton went four innings and gave up a couple of runs. Afterward, McCarver was in the washroom with some other veterans, and Carlton approached him. "Lefty came over and said, 'Hey'—he didn't call me by my name," McCarver said later. "'Hey, you've got to call more breaking pitches when we're behind the hitter.' Well, that really blew my mind. I backed him up against the wall and said, 'You sonofabitch. You got a lot of guts telling me that. What credentials do you have?' Lefty turned red, as he often does. The next day we both felt bad. I apologized, but he didn't." They've disagreed on almost everything since then—and gotten along famously. The only quality they seem to have in common is total honesty with each other.

The relationship helped prolong McCarver's career. Af-

had my last hurrah when I came back for Carlton," he says. "To come back and prove something to people who had written me off was my greatest thrill."

Maybe that's why McCarver takes such an upbeat view of the way Carlton is going out. Released by the Phillies this season, he played briefly for the Giants, then went to the White Sox. "People say you should go gracefully when the team tells you to," says McCarver. "That's B.S. You're taught to compete. I think you should have the uniform torn off you. People say that's sad. It's not sad; it's just a downside. At least Steve is going out on his own terms. And imagine the satisfaction if he comes back."

Ah, but Carlton is fighting the inevitable; McCarver prepared for it. A decade before his retirement, he was becoming a full man: a cover-to-cover newspaper reader ("The best place to find first sections is in the clubhouse, where they're unopened, brand-spanking-new, because the players take the sports sections"), an oenophile, a sharp bridge player, a business student at Memphis State. No one was surprised when the Phils hired him as a radio and TV commentator for the 1980 season.

"He actually talked too much, unlike most guys up from the field," says Phillie broadcaster Harry Kalas, Pennsylvania Sportscaster of the Year from 1980 to 1985. As a "color" man complementing the play-by-play announcer, McCarver at first belittled his own playing career, a la Bob Uecker and Joe Garagiola.

Eventually, Kalas convinced him that his humble-pie act wasn't natural, and McCarver's knowledge and enthusiasm began to work for him. (He occasionally regresses, as at the 1986 All-Star Game, when Al Michaels had to drag out of him the fact that he himself had batted 1.000 in his two All-Star appearances.)

One person watching closely was Mets senior vice president Al Harazin. '"This city was ripe for someone to come on the scene and be a star," he says. "A lot of ex-players know the game, but we felt Timmy could make it entertaining and interesting." Harazin hired McCarver after the 1982 season.

Kiner and Zabriskie handled the middle three innings. Despite McCarver's warning, Zane Smith, the Atlanta pitcher, threw a 3–2 curve with the bases loaded. George Foster doubled to put the Mets ahead 5–0. McCarver's presence was felt even when McCarver wasn't present.

When McCarver returned, Ojeda was finishing a 5–1 win by throwing three different types of change-ups and befuddling the Atlanta batters. Next inning, the poem McCarver had been toying with, "The Pitcher," was duly flashed on the screen. "That poem was written by Yogi Berra, back in 1952," joked McCarver. He went on to compare Ojeda's performance to the poem, and to relay Webster's definition of arrant: "Being notoriously without moderation, extreme." McCarver's eyes twinkled behind his glasses. Describing a fly ball, he said, "Well hit to left field, but not arrant enough."

"That's the thing about broadcasting," McCarver said between innings. "Try anything, even if it doesn't work." That must explain "the incredibly stupid stat," an innovation dreamed up by McCarver and Bill Webb. In past games, viewers have been informed that umpire Doug Harvey had brushed off the plate 17 times through seven innings and that third base coach Buddy Harrelson had kicked the bag 38 times. Now Zabriskie, reading in his best Lone Ranger Intro voice, intoned, "Once again, as America waits breathlessly next to their television sets all over the nation, it's time for the incredibly stupid stat of tonight's game."

McCarver: "Through eight innings, Keith Hernandez has kicked first base a total of 32 times. ... Now here's video to back it up." Mets first baseman Keith Hernandez is shown kicking the bag twice.

The game ended in a quick two hours, 22 minutes. Glasses off for an on-camera shot, McCarver assisted Kiner with the wrap-up. Over a martini in the press dining room, he was bubbling. The broadcast had been short and sweet. Everything had worked. "It

out of cup-holders on the side. "Nice to meet you," he said.

McCarver looked grimly at him. "We haven't been introduced yet," he said evenly.

"What a distorted idea of celebrity we have in this country," McCarver said as he reached the car. The seat-belt warning signal sounded: boing, boing, boing, boing. "Charming fellow, wasn't he? Those are D and D guys—distance and darkness. Put them in between you as fast as you can. If you handle them with honesty, not abruptness, it works out."

(His celebrity likely won't be diminished by Esquire magazine's choice of a model for the cover of its fashion issue this month: There's McCarver, right out front, grinning gamefully in an $850 double-breasted pinstripe suit.)

Back in Manhattan, McCarver headed to his favorite neighborhood bistro for dinner. Unfortunately, the kitchen had closed. Baseball men can relate dozens of these experiences. In an effort to live a more normal life during his final years as a player, McCarver stopped returning to Memphis each winter and moved his family to Philadelphia. His wife, Ann, and his daughters, Kathy, 20, a senior at Virginia, and Kelly, 18, who is headed to the University of Vermont, have remained in Philadelphia through the daughters' high school years. The McCarvers are considering a move to New York in the next few years.

"I enjoy the winters at home more than ever now. I'm more a work-hard-and-enjoy-it person than a make-it-while-you-can. Someone once said that when you look forward to your next haircut, you're in trouble. The demands of this job are great. I don't want to be a workaholic at the expense of everything else."

Earlier in his broadcast career, McCarver was sounded out about managing the Expos or general managing the Cardinals. He subsequently re-upped with the Mets and is now on the second year of a four-year contract. "I don't want to do anything else," he said, sucking on a Belgian beer. "This is a lot more relaxing than playing or managing. Players who say they don't take the game home and throw it at the wife — that's B.S. Almost everyone does if they care: You have to live the game. But you don't as a broadcaster. I don't have to take the game home with me."

He smiled and savored the irony. This had been one game he was only too happy to take home.

[McCarver went on to a spectacular career on nationwide TV and covered a record number of World Series games. Now semi-retired in Sarasota, Florida, he still broadcasts some Cardinal games.]

CHAPTER EIGHT

Number Nine On Your Scorecard. . .

of baseball's most enigmatic figures. In the sandlots he's either left out or last chosen. He's the little kid exiled from second base, the fat boy expelled from catcher, the slow boat moved over from center. Not until he reaches the majors does he attain his singular stature: lord of sunlight and nightlight, master of carom and corner, longbowman with the on-target arm. Yet he remains little noted nor long remembered, number nine on our scorecards and last in our hearts.

Every so often baseball perks up and takes notice of the position. Such a year was 1984, when the Padres' Tony Gwynn led the majors in hitting; the Cubs' Keith Moreland and the Tigers' Kirk Gibson made critical playoff catches; and Gibson added a key throw and two decisive homers in the Series. And the hottest new player anywhere was a right fielder. Guy named Hobbs. Roy Hobbs. They called him The Natural.

As it happens, naturals have long abounded in right field. There are 20 right fielders in the Hall of Fame—more than any other position but pitcher. Among these immortals are Babe Ruth, Hank Aaron, Mel Ott, Paul Waner, Frank Robinson, Al Kaline and the peerless gloveman Roberto Clemente.

How could the weakest position in amateur ball become the strongest in major-league history? "In organized ball you're going to have good hitters in right," says Kaline. "Up-the-middle players—catcher short, second and center—concentrate on their fielding. The other players—first, third, left and right—can concentrate more on their hitting." The right fielder usually makes baseball's longest throw—as long as 450 feet from deepest right to third in the old Polo Grounds. The player with the strongest arm should also hit for the most power.

But the explanation isn't all that pat. Tricky to learn and tough to play, right demands an especially resilient athlete. He makes more difficult throws than any other outfielder, and the throw is an outfielder's greatest challenge. "Catching a fly ball is a pleasure," Yankees' great Tommy Henrich used to say, "but knowing what to do with it after you make the catch is a business."

No one has to know—or do—more than a right fielder. When a ball bounces near the line, for example, right-handed right fielders must execute a back-to-the-plate pivot before throwing to second. All right fielders must catch flies in perfect position to throw out runners tagging at second. "The right fielder has to keep runners from advancing more than any other player does," says former Baltimore right fielder Ken Singleton.

There is no outfield scene as taut and tense as the sight of a right fielder charging a base hit as a runner rounds second. The pickup and pivot and peg must be perfect. When he succeeds, there's an epic, almost surreal quality to his throw. From Enos Slaughter cutting down Tuck Stainback in the 1942 Series to George Hendrick nabbing Robin Yount in 1982, right fielders have made throws to third that resembled 300-foot clotheslines strung across the sky.

* * *

The master of the art was Clemente. As a high-school player in Puerto Rico, he switched from shortstop to the outfield. When he was 18, the Dodgers were conducting a tryout at Sixto Escobar Stadium in San Juan. "The first thing I did was ask kids to throw from the outfield," says Al Campanis, the player-personnel vice president of the Dodgers. "This kid Clemente throws a bullet from center, on the fly. '¡*Uno Más!*' I shout, and he does it again." The Dodgers eventually signed Clemente for a $10,000 bonus, left him unprotected on their Montreal farm club and lost him in the draft to the Pirates. As a big-league right fielder from 1955 to 1972, he won 12 Gold Gloves and a National-League-record 5 assist titles. Players referred to his arm as El Bazooka.

"Orlando Cepeda of the Giants hit a line drive down the runway and past the bullpen, which was behind the stands and out of sight in Forbes Field," recalls Phil Dorsey, a Clemente confidant.

set metal baskets on their sides at second and third," says Dorsey. "A coach would hit balls off the screen above the right-field wall [in play], and Roberto would work for hours retrieving them and throwing them into the baskets."

"I've watched tapes of Clemente," says the Cardinals' Andy Van Slyke, one of the National League's best defensive right fielders. "He loved it when a guy challenged him. I try to be like that. I always charge the ball. Sometimes I'll bobble it, and the runner will take an extra base. So what? If I hadn't been aggressive, he'd be there anyway. There's nothing like the outfielder who tells the runner, 'I dare you to run.'"

Hence, the profile of the ideal right fielder: aggressive, confident, even cocky. When the Yankees' Rickey Henderson reaches first on a Toronto pitcher, he'll sometimes turn around toward right fielder Jesse Barfield, shake his legs and smile: I'm going. Barfield, who led all right fielders with 22 assists in 1985, responds by blowing on the index finger like a gunslinger clearing smoke from a six-gun: You're a dead man. "Some runners will tell me to back up and give them a chance," says Barfield. "I tell them, 'no way—don't even try.'" If they're foolish enough to go, Barfield is prepared. Before games he and shortstop Tony Fernandez play "long-toss," a 200-foot game of catch that helps them strengthen their arms and lengthen their throws. Barfield and center fielder Lloyd Moseby also play a baseball-style "21" in which they throw to each other from 50 feet. "If he catches my throws at his belt buckle," I get one point," says Barfield. "Two for the chest; three for the head. You get in the habit of hitting the target."

* * *

The challenging throw isn't all that ennobles the right fielder. It's accepted that fly balls come relatively straight at center fielders but tend to hook or slice toward the lines in right or left. Well, the English on the ball can be considerably weirder on a right fielder than a left fielder. Most balls hit to left fielders are thrown by right-handed pitchers and batted by right-handers. When a pitcher throws the ball, it's likely to come at a batter with left-to-right spin; the batter hits it with a right-to-left motion. The ball may still move crazily off the bat, but the countervailing movements are likely to straighten it out a bit. Balls hit to right are usually thrown by right-handers and hit by left-handers: two left-to-right motions producing wicked hooks. "It comes at you like a banana," says Detroit right fielder Pat Sheridan.

But not always. "The ball doesn't curve toward the line every time because some right-handed hitters can drive it up the gap," says Keith Moreland. Adds Boston's Dwight Evans: "Three batters would give me fits. Tony Oliva's drives would hook or sink or rise over my head—he made me feel like a fool. Cecil Cooper hits balls that take off to my right; you don't see that from other left-handed hitters. Graig Nettles would hit balls with topspin and bite. I'd think they'd be easy catches and I'd wind up diving."

No wonder right fielders work so hard at getting a jump on the ball. "My speed wasn't a factor in my fielding—my jump was," says Rusty Staub, who played right for much of his 23-year baseball career. "When I came up to the Astros, a coach, Jim Busby, taught me how to get a jump. He'd hit me line drive after line drive from 150 feet. Eventually I'd learn how to see the ball off the bat. Then Busby would lengthen out his hits. I did everything I could to know the pitchers and hitters. I'd talk to the catcher about how he'd call the game; and while it was in progress I'd get signals from the catcher, shortstop or second baseman."

The right fielder's worst enemy may be boredom. Since he touches the ball far less than anyone else—most hitters are right-handed—he constantly fights the urge to daydream. "I expect the ball to be hit to me 27 times a game," says Van Slyke. "That's how I keep my head in the game. I keep asking myself questions: 'If the ball's hit down the line, is Keith Hernandez or Mookie Wilson

all the time. In right, you might go four games without a chance, but then you might get one with a game on the line." Moreland now feels at home in Wrigley, one of the most pernicious—and the only perennial—sun field. Brewer right fielder Charlie Moore, another converted catcher, says, "I keep awake by talking either to myself or the center fielder: 'I'll cheat by the line, so come by me.' As catcher I used to go crazy seeing balls drop in front of the outfielders. As a result, I play in close and work on the fewer balls that are hit over my head. I also have a pretty good idea how we'll pitch the hitters. I look out where our catchers are setting up, and I guess what they're calling. As I guess, I cheat a little on my left or right."

All right fielders share the awareness that theirs can be an un-forgiving position. Waiting for plays—and, remember, they wait longer than anyone in the game—they wonder what will go wrong. And something unfortunate, even ludicrous, happens all to often.

Kirk Gibson, after being tutored by Al Kaline, made an excel-lent throw to help the Tigers win the first 1984 Series game. "A year ago I would have thrown a screwball," he said. A day later Gibson made an error. Tony Gwynn spent the 1984 season build-ing a reputation as a competent fielder. Then he helped allow the go-ahead run in the final Series game by losing a fly ball in the lights. In 1982, Moreland dove for a ball, got up and couldn't find it. The ball was lying in his cap. It could have happened any-where; it happened in right.

Back in 1934, Hall of Fame center fielder Hack Wilson was winding down his career as a right fielder with Casey Stengel's Brooklyn Dodgers. The hard-drinking Wilson, "hung over like a cornice," in the words of the late Red Smith, was running down line drives off Brooklyn's appropriately named Boom Boom Beck. Each time Stengel visited the mound to change pitchers, Beck talked him out of it.

Finally, after one line drive too many, Stengel stormed to the mound and demanded the ball. Furious beyond words, Beck wheeled and threw it to deep right. Wilson, who had been leaning against the fence and dozing, heard the familiar rattle of ball against fence. He wheeled, fielded the carom, and fired a strike to second. "That was the best throw Hack made all year," Stengel said later. Wilson could have been hung over anywhere; he was hung over in right.

* * *

By all odds, right field has the most colorful history of any outfield position. At first, it was the weakest spot on the diamond. There were few left-handed batters, and pitchers threw so slowly that most balls were hit to center or left. The man placed in right was often the "change" pitcher, an early term for reliever, since teams were forbidden to substitute from the bench. Hall of Fame pitcher Old Hoss Radbourn spent an afternoon in right and won an 18-innig game with a homer.

Another oddity: Right tended to be the "short" field and shallow-situated right fielders could always hope for 9–3 assists. On June 12, 1880, Worcester rightfielder Lon Knight threw to first baseman Chub Sullivan to retire Cleveland batter Bill Phillips and help J. Lee Richmond throw baseball's first perfect game. The 9–3 phenomenon faded in the Sixties when outfields became much larger, though the Cardinals' Van Slyke reprised it in spring training this year, throwing out former Atlanta pitcher Len Barker on a one-hop liner.

In 1891, free substitutions were permitted and teams stopped using pitchers in right. One of the leading right fielders of the time, the Phillies' Big Sam Thompson, changed outfield play forever by perfecting the one-bounce throw home; previously, outfielders usually threw only as far as the infield. The Red Sox' Harry Hooper, probably the best fielding right fielder of the first half of the century, set an unofficial mark for his position with 344 career assists and invented the "rump-slide," in which he threw himself to the ground on one hip, feet forward, knees bent, while catching short fly balls.

friendly fan. Their protest was not upheld by the umpire, but the debate would rage for some 50 years. In 1965, Rice gave the Hall of Fame a sealed letter to be opened upon his death. He died in 1974. In the letter, Rice said he had a "death grip" on the ball but while falling into the stands "hit my Adam's apple or something, which sort of knocked me out for a few seconds. At no time," Rice insisted, "did I lose possession of the ball."

At no time did the thrills slacken in right. The selfless Kaline once made a game-saving catch while breaking his shoulder. Heartbreak? To many students of right there's none greater than seeing the late Roger Maris left out of the Hall. Forget about his seven World Series, two Most Valuable Player awards and one mythical asterisk. He was a great defensive right fielder: Just ask Willie Mays, deprived of a game-tying RBI in the last inning of the 1962 World Series, when Maris went into the corner to cut off his double.

If right field torments, it can also bless. The normally lead-footed Lou Piniella somehow came up with two critical plays in the Yankees' epic 1978 playoff victory over the Red Sox. First, he made a running grab that robbed Fred Lynn of a double; and then he feigned the catch of a Jerry Remy fly he lost in the sun. Another habitual cold glove, the Mets' Ron Swoboda made the diving catch that saved game four of the 1969 World Series.

* * *

The greatest catch of the greatest game in World Series history, however, was made by Boston's Dwight Evans, the nonpareil right fielder of the post-Clemente era and possibly the last of a noble breed.

The old right fields had varying dimensions, screens, fences, walls, funny angles and crazy caroms. And because the ball moved slowly on grass, the right fielder of yore was better known for the quality of his arm than his speed. The new parks usually have artificial turf, walls 8 to 12 feet high and uniform dimensions (typically, 330 feet to the poles and 400 to dead center). True, the turf forces the right fielder to station himself deeper than he'd like to and continue to make deep throws. However, the carpet also creates faster hits up the gaps. When most managers are forced to choose between fast legs and strong arms—they infrequently get a player with both—they're tempted to opt for speed.

The 1985 Royal and Cardinal outfields, to name two, were stocked end to end with players of center field speed. Oh, there are still some right fielders built along he classic lines—Minnesota's Tom Brunansky, Cincinnati's Dave Parker and Toronto's Barfield come to mind—but they're wasted on phony turf. For an old-fashioned right fielder and an old-fashioned right field, we look to Evans.

Like his distinguished predecessors—among them Hooper, Jimmy Piersall and Jackie Jensen—Evans has grown accustomed to playing baseball's toughest right field. In Fenway, right is a sinister sun field—especially so since the rays shine in a fielder's eyes over the low grandstand. There are hockey-style caroms off a curved corner, or "belly," beginning 302 feet from the plate and extending to 380. The right-field fence never rises to 6 feet, so balls are more likely to be over it than off it. And there's virtually no foul ground, so any ball hit a right fielder's way is likely to be trouble. Nonetheless, Evans learned to play right so well he once went 191 consecutive games without making an error.

Consider him in practice. Other players are clowning around, standing in groups with their hats on backwards, making off-balance catches, throwing their gloves at the ball. Evans practices the way he plays. A coach hits him 10 minutes of grounders and he comes up throwing with each. "You have to charge the ball, slow up a little before you get to it, and try to get a good hop," he says. "Then make a curve around the ball, so that you're lined up in the direction you want to throw." Evans makes the play as well

ball. Immediately, Evans felt dread—he'll probably pull the ball and hit it over my head. And, sure enough, Morgan produced an outfielder's nightmare—a liner streaking over Evans's head like a guided missile, with some left-to-right English thrown in.

Unlike the flashy players who misjudge balls, get late starts and have to dive, Evans prides himself on making his best catches look easy. Sizing up the shot, he retreated quickly, eyes on the ball, and stabbed it at the warning track. "Given its significance," said shocked Cincinnati manager Sparky Anderson, "it was one of the two greatest catches ever made."

But like all great outfielders, Evans wasn't satisfied with making the catch. "I think my best plays have been good throws," he says. "Making a good throw gives me the same feeling as hitting a homer." Bouncing off the wall and throwing toward a crowd of Boston uniforms in the infield, Evans didn't make his best throw. No matter; his quick release more than atoned for his imperfect aim. First baseman Carl Yastrzemski caught the ball some 25 feet from the bag and relayed it to shortstop Rick Burleson, who had crossed the diamond to reach first well ahead of Griffey. It was a 9–3–6 double play if you're scoring, and a play that had fans, television viewers and even sportswriters embracing and shouting, if you're remembering.

It could have happened anywhere; it happened in right.

CHAPTER NINE

Talkin' Baseball

I've been studying baseball for most of my 72 years, feeling all the while that I have much to learn about it. There's always another leaf to be lifted; and beneath it lie new disclosures, theories, facts, surprises, analysis and strategy of this ever-evolving sport. During the seasons, people are involved with action on the field. The time for a potpourri of revelation is afterward.

The Hot Stove League is the three-and-a-half month interval between the end of the World Series around November 1 and the February 15 date when the pitchers and catchers report to spring training in Arizona and Florida. Traditionally, men would gather around hot stoves and talk baseball. Aside from speculating over possible trades, there wasn't much else to discuss.

All that has changed. As Peter Gammons has observed, high salaries, free agency and the news they generate have made baseball topical 12 months a year. Everything from talk radio and TV to the MLB channel, newspapers, magazines and innumerable blogs keep conversation, argumentation and insight bubbling all winter. Endless tidbits of new information, speculation, and debate abound.

I love attending live, cold-weather events where baseball people hold forth, and I was fortunate to witness two of them in four days of January 2016. There's no way to flesh out all the issues, anecdotes and trivia discussed, many of which could fill whole winter evenings or Saturday afternoons. They were soupçons of larger issues, tasty treats to enjoy with further study.

On January 15 I drove to Northfield, Massachusetts for the annual Hot Stove League event at Northfield Mount Hermon School. The impressive panel of active baseball personnel included Buster Olney of ESPN (a graduate of the school); Galen Carr, the

Dodgers' director of player personnel; Oliver Drake, an Orioles pitcher and another NMH grad; Todd Radom, a uniform and logo designer; and Gus Quattlebaum, the Red Sox' director of pro scouting. Three days later, I accompanied baseball historians John S. Bowman and Duke Goldman to a Society for American Research (SABR) event at the Baseball Tavern outside Fenway

Naval Academy alum got the call from the Orioles and was told to call the traveling secretary for flight information. With no sleep, he packed and flew to Miami, where the Orioles were playing an interleague game with the Marlins. Drake knew the Orioles wore suits on the road but mistakenly left his on the plane. After suffering visions of himself in jeans, a rookie eyesore, he got permission to re-board the craft and grab his suit bag. Whew!

Drake had always consumed peanut-butter-and-jelly sandwiches before games; but veteran Delmon Young informed him, "We've got good food here."

Drake warmed up several times in his first game as an Oriole and finally got the call to start the ninth inning of a scoreless game. His adrenaline spiking, he flew to the mound and immediately threw two balls. Gathering himself, Drake settled down and retired the side in order. In the 10th he found himself with runners on second and third, with two outs, and threw a potentially game-ending wild pitch by his catcher. Drake rushed to the plate, got the throw and tagged out the runner. Marlins manager Dan Jennings protested. Following a two-minute review, the call was upheld. Whew! Drake threw a third scoreless inning before bowing out. He celebrated afterward with his parents and girlfriend. In 13 appearances with the Orioles, he has a 2.87 ERA and was looking forward to the 2016 season.

With all due respect to the other panelists, Olney carried the evening. His candor was remarkable. Olney stopped voting for Hall of Famers out of disgust. There were 17 legitimate candidates in the last election, he said; however, voters could select only 10 of them. Why shouldn't Roger Clemens and Barry Bonds be inducted despite their almost certain use of performance-enhancing drugs [when they played]? "The game was saturated with PEDs," Olney said, "so you're going to say retroactively they're bad? Players who did it were competing against players who did it. Put it on their plaques [if necessary]."

Olney pointed out that Clemens, Bonds and Mark McGwire are employed by major-league franchises and by inference in good standing. He hoped the election of Mike Piazza, suspected of PED use, would be "the tipping point." Olney went on: "I can't stand the demonization of individual players. The guy who put in the character clause [for HOF eligibility] was [Commissioner] Kennesaw Mountain Landis, who in his last years was trying to keep baseball segregated."

Perhaps owing to advancing age, I've been convinced by the last intelligent argument I heard on the subject. So I was leaning toward forgiveness of the best players in the steroid era. I respect the arguments of those who vote no on steroid-tainted candidates, but I urge them to grant an exception to players who tested positive only in 2003. Those findings were supposed to be secret but got leaked. That means David Ortiz should be elected to Cooperstown in his first year of eligibility.

Olney wasn't reluctant to criticize his working peers. The Baseball Writers' Association of America doesn't release individual ballots, "incredible for a business involved in openness." On December 6, 2016, the BBWAA voted to release all individual ballots. Olney also worried that too many writers are employed by teams or Major League Baseball, implying that there isn't enough critical coverage. He blasted teams like the Braves and Reds for what he charged as "tanking"—purposely finishing low in the standings to get high draft picks—"a level of consumer fraud."

There were delicious trends and predictions spread over the two-hour session. Hitters may stop working the count, the panel agreed. What's the point in wearing out the starting pitcher when he'll be gone after five or six innings anyway? Hitters don't mind pitchers illegally using pine tar and sunscreen on their hands, according to the night's consensus, because it improves their accuracy and batter safety. Look for more good players from South Korea. You want a job in baseball? Be prepared to spend several

There was more. Successful players are superconfident: Derek Jeter, Tony Gwynn and Mariano Rivera were convinced they'd win every game. Olney said that a current wunderkind, Bryce Harper, could get a $500-million contract from the Yankees when he qualifies for free agency. The Cubs will beat the Royals in the 2016 World Series, Olney said, to friendly boos.

If that crowd was filled with feet-on-the-ground baseball insiders, the SABR meeting three days later, at the Baseball Tavern in sight of Fenway Park, included many elderly men who have spent years analyzing the game and crunching numbers. But they aren't the kind of numbers that make your eyes glaze over. One of the speakers, Andy Andres, a senior lecturer in natural sciences at Boston University, argued that the popular WAR (Wins Over Replacement Player) is not a precise measure of excellence. For one thing, it's tough to calculate fielding excellence. A guy with a good fielding percentage may not get to as many balls as a player who makes some errors but covers huge swaths of turf. Andres noted that right fielders are judged on the same plane as left fielders, even though their throws to third are longer than virtually anything left fielders routinely face.

And how do you evaluate base running, which isn't just stolen bases but skill in going from first to third or second to home on a single, or crossing the plate on a wild pitch. "WAR is fuzzy, like referees placing the ball in football," Andres concluded.

A man in the audience filling a level of seats a few feet below the bar said David Ortiz was more valuable to the Red Sox as a designated hitter than Derek Jeter was to the Yankees late in his career. "Jeter cost the Yankees runs as a fielder and Ortiz didn't," he argued. "Ortiz is an incredibly good hitter. Watching him is on the same plane as watching Larry Bird play basketball."

More speakers followed a lunch of salad, hot dogs, sausages, meatball and chicken fragments. Gordon Edes, late a reporter of the Boston Globe and ESPN, spoke about his new job as Red Sox historian. He's well qualified. Edes wondered: If the Red Sox hadn't traded the black pitcher Earl Wilson in 1966 after he complained of being denied service in a Florida bar, would the one-two punch of Jim Lonborg and Wilson have been enough to beat the Cardinals in the 1967 World Series? And if Ted Williams hadn't been hurt in an exhibition series the Red Sox played late in the 1946 season, would they have beaten the Cardinals in another Fall Classic? On reflection, I wondered about the absences of Tony Conigliaro in the '67 Series and Jim Rice in '75.

Alex Speier of the Boston Globe said that Hall of Fame voters over-emphasize batting average at the expense of on-base percentage, citing Lou Whitaker (.363 OBP), Bobby Grich (.371) and Dwight Evans (.370), who were dropped off the ballot when they didn't get the required 5% in their first three years on the ballot. Speier argued for "less vituperation and more dialogue" in baseball analysis. He said the two most important innovations in baseball journalism are the "Moneyball" ideology, which he defined as intellectual openness, and the www.baseball-reference.com play index, which allows users to follow an intricate path through a player's or many players' careers.

Here's where I followed up. With Gabriel Schechter's help I went into the free play index area for Dwight Evans, one of my favorite players, and got a complete rundown of all 1,384 of his RBI: when, against which pitcher, which park, what game situation. He had three leading off games, 10 game-ending, 278 go-ahead, 109 tying, 10 walk-off. This is what Casey Stengel called "deep depth." Registering for a $2, 24-hour subscription to the deeper play index, I found Patrick Languzzi making a case for

Evans's Hall-of-Fame credentials. Languzzi noted that Evans led the American League in homers (256) during the 1980s and all of baseball in runs created (1,067) and extra-base hits (605) during the decade. The index also included historian Bill James's open letter to the Hall of Fame making the case for Evans. James wrote that players who do many things well get less attention than those who do one thing spectacularly well. That was Evans. In one of

Clemente. That alone would justify his induction for this fielding maven. Surely his catch of Joe Morgan's blast that helped the Red Sox win Game Six of the 1975 World Series established Evans as a fielding legend. In any case, offense alone should have kept him on the HOF ballot more than his three years.

A SABR star, Bill Nowlin, gave a talk on the Boston Braves' Sam Jethroe, first black player in the Hub when he was signed for the 1950 season. One can only imagine the racist razzing he might have received in Fenway Park. At Braves Field, however, the lunch pail crowd shouted, "Go, Sam, Go!" He stole a league-leading 35 bases along with 18 homers and a .278 average, and was elected National League Rookie of the Year.

The final speaker we heard, Donna Halper, described how Bostonians followed baseball before radio was introduced. Crowds of 50–60,000 people would gather on Newspaper Row to hear updates by megaphones and wait for papers, which sometimes had seven editions. There were jugglers and clowns, musicians and singers performing. It was quite a show.

As were those two meetings in four January days.

Did you seriously expect me to miss SABR Day? Occurring on January 30, between the NFL title games and the Super Bowl, SABR Day features meetings at chapters all over the country. I drove to Middlesex Community College in Middletown, Connecticut, because I knew that continuing discussion over the Hall of Fame would be on the agenda.

The two guest speakers were Connecticut sportswriter Dave Borges, who voted in the Hall of Fame election for the first time, and Bob Wirz, whom I knew from his days as publicist for the Kansas City Royals and later the commissioner. Borges said the Hall wouldn't be complete without Roger Clemens and Barry Bonds, virtually certain PED use notwithstanding; and he also voted for users McGwire and Sosa. Wirz, just stripped of his right to vote by eligibility streamlining, left the four off his ballot because of their suspect character failings.

Someone wondered if character questions had kept anyone from being elected before the steroid era. One suggestion: Carl Mays, who had almost the same record as Hall-of-Famer Bob Lemon (207–126, 2.92 ERA to 207–128, 3.23 ERA) but also threw the pitch that killed Ray Chapman in 1920. You could also make a case for Maury Wills, the Gold Glove-winning Dodger shortstop who revitalized steals as an offensive weapon with 586 of them but had an alcohol and cocaine problem. Bill James rated Wills baseball's 19th best shortstop. Of course, plenty of racists, drunks and wife beaters have plaques in Cooperstown. "Anyone who knows anything about [the] character [issue] knows it's bull," said Alan Cohen, one of the Middletown organizers.

Wirz was flabbergasted that Carlos Delgado, who had 30+ homers 10 years in a row, lasted just one year on the ballot. He further questioned the information voters are given on player ballots. "Some of those things they highlight are pathetic," he said.

The mention of Pete Rose's name in the discussion of Hall qualifications brought universal laughter; but Wirz pointed out, "In my years of involvement, there was never a player who came closer to understanding where he stood and where his peers stood than Pete Rose. I give him full credit for that."

At meeting's end, I met Marjorie Adams, a bright and energetic woman plugging her great-grandfather Doc Adams for the Hall. Many historians think Adams, who created and popularized the shortstop position and headed the 1857 commission that established basic rules like nine men to a side, nine innings to a

game and 90 feet between bases, trumps the largely discredited
Alexander Cartwright as the Father of Baseball. In the 2015
election for pre-integration Famers, Adams headed the list with
10 votes. Unfortunately, he needed 12 of the 16 possible votes to
qualify. When I looked up his web site, I found official baseball
historian John Thorn praising Adams and mourning that the
last two pre-integration elections failed to appoint

CHAPTER TEN

My Turn

Now I get to do some hyperventilating on my own. Please be advised that the criticisms I'm about to issue are meant to be constructive. And once you finish reading them, you'll be rewarded with praise for the national pastime.

Some of baseball's stick-in-the-mud practices, well, stick in the mud. It seems harmless enough when a player hits one out, then flips his bat overhead in celebration. Yet the pitcher involved and his team may take offense, even to the point of saying the batter was "pimping," then hitting the offensive batter with the next opportunity. Really. Peter Abraham of the *Boston Globe* has an appropriate response: "Baseball needs to get out of the 1950s. Celebrating a home run or pumping your fist should not lead to some cranky redneck pitcher trying to injure you with a fastball next time you're up.

"High school and college players flip bats and have all sorts of fun, as do players in Caribbean and Asian leagues [and many African-Americans]." A contributor to *The New York Times Magazine* referred to baseball's straight-laced traditions as "racially coded." That's unfair—"antiquated" would be more accurate.

"The unwritten rules need to be thrown out," Abraham continued. "If pitchers hate celebrations so much, throw better pitches. Baseball is determined to appeal to a younger age demographic and allowing celebrations would help that. The world will keep spinning."

Steve Buckley of the *Boston Herald* seconded that thought: "In the interest of disclosure, I'm an old-school baseball writer who thinks it's fine that Ortiz pimps his home runs. Baseball needs more of this, not less. If Gronk can spike the ball after a touchdown; if hockey players can do an en masse hug after a goal has been scored; if basketball players can hang like a chandelier after a dunk; if soccer players can practically undress after putting the ball in the net; then it should be O.K. for guys like David Ortiz and Jose Bautista to hotdog it with liberal doses of mustard after hitting a home run."

And while we're at it, baseball needs to stop enforcing its

platform that allows athletes to speak directly to fans without the impediment of those ink-stained wretches in the press box. Jeter and David Ortiz announced their retirements on TPT, and athletes from other sports have signed onto the masthead. The last time I checked, Ortiz was listed as Editor at Large, Tiger Woods as Contributing Editor, Kobe Bryant as Editorial Director and Matt Harvey as New York City Bureau Chief. Seriously.

Look, I can understand why players struggling with English may need help (every club has a Spanish-language translator); and others may recoil when words they didn't mean to say appear in print or elsewhere. But in the end TPT is a meretricious vehicle, an end run around the media and the public they seek to serve with intelligent reporting and analysis. It may be the first step toward players clamming up altogether, except by news release.

While I'm foaming at the mouth, I'm also aghast at the fact that ballplayers who became millionaires thanks to a union as well as their personal excellence too often vote for the anti-union party. Players would rather complain about their high taxes than go to bat for decent, honest, hard-working, regular, rock-bed Americans getting the short end of the stick.

And what about race? Race? Isn't that where baseball made a seminal contribution to society in the person of Jackie Robinson? Yes, but where was the follow-up? By the end of the 1953 season, after seven full years of integration, only four of the eight American League teams (Chicago White Sox, St. Louis Browns, Cleveland Indians and Philadelphia Athletics) and four of the eight National League teams (Boston Braves, Brooklyn Dodgers, New York Giants and Chicago Cubs) had fielded black players. Unofficial quotas limited numbers on teams that did integrate; that's one theory why the Dodgers didn't protect Roberto Clemente and lost him to the Pirates. (The other theory was that they were "hiding" him.)

It took 28 years before Frank Robinson became the first black manager with the 1975 Indians, and every few years baseball people note how few minority skippers there are. Toward the end of the 2015 season, there was just one: Cuban-born Fredi González of the Atlanta Braves (who was fired in 2016!). Soon after, the Dodgers hired Dave Roberts, who has an African-American father and a Japanese mother; and the Washington Nationals chose the African-American Dusty Baker. It's been said that baseball tends to hire managers from the "buddy system." If so, why aren't there more blacks included in that culture? The game's only African-American general managers in 2016 were Michael Hill of the Miami Marlins and Dave Stewart of the Arizona Diamondbacks, the latter fired at season's end. Kenny Williams is team president of the Chicago White Sox. Owners? Please. The dearth of black players is even more discomforting. Opening Day rosters and disabled lists in 2016 showed just 8% of players are Americans who identified themselves as black or African-American, including 1.3% of the pitchers. That's well down from the high-water mark of 19% in 1986, according to research by Mark Armour of the Society for American Baseball Research (SABR).

Now, some innocuous explanations have been put forth. White American representation is also down, thanks to the influx of athletes from the Caribbean Basin—many of them black—and Asia. A black kid growing up in an American inner city will learn at a young age whether or not he has game enough for a basketball scholarship. An African-American youngster in some rural town will sense whether or not he's tough enough for a football scholarship. With its skills so subtle and elusive, baseball offers no such promise; in fact, the costs of special coaching and travel to showcase events are a disincentive to planning a future in the national pastime. The problem for young African-Americans may begin at birth. If baseball is fathers playing catch with sons (thank you, Donald Hall), two-thirds of black women with kids are single mothers. The suggestion is that sons don't get coaching. That

American executive and scout, the RBI (Reviving Baseball in Inner Cities) program has served more than 230,000 athletes in 200 cities; and the Washington Nationals opened a Youth Baseball Academy last year. Seven blacks were first-round draft picks in 2015, the highest number since 1992; and ESPN's Keith Law rated 14 black players, including three of the top seven, among the 100 best prospects. But in 2016 only four of the top 100 minor-league prospects, according to the MLB.com ranking, are blacks. If their numbers on major-league rosters are low, they seem to have stabilized around 8% since 2010. Still, we need more black players, and not just because it's the right thing to do. Haven't some of baseball's greatest leaders been blacks like Frank Robinson, some of the best teammates African-Americans like David Price; some of the most inspiring figures people of color like Hank Aaron? And wouldn't we like to see more black fans at the park?

My own personal, almost frenzied pet peeve about baseball is the exclusion of Marvin Miller from the Hall of Fame. In a serious embarrassment for baseball, a 2007 committee charged with inducting executives chose former commissioner Bowie Kuhn over Miller. When Miller's name again came up three years later, he fell one vote short.

We will get to Mr. Kuhn in a minute. It's widely felt that the three most important figures in modern baseball history were

Babe Ruth, Jackie Robinson and Marvin Miller. With low salaries and a ban on freely changing teams, ballplayers were exploited before Miller became executive director of the Major League Baseball Players' Association in 1966. Through a series of strikes, litigation, arbitration and hard bargaining, the Miller years gave players salary arbitration after three full seasons, free agency after six, and salaries that averaged $4.25 million, with a minimum of $507,500, in 2015. In 1966, the average was $17,644; and the minimum $7,000.

At the Middletown SABR meeting from the last chapter, Bob Wirz asked of Miller, "What did he do to support and improve baseball?" A meeting organizer, Steve Krevisky, citing his union membership, replied: "Miller changed the game in ways some didn't like but improved it in terms of rights for players."

After the meeting, I was discussing the matter with baseball author Bill Ryczek. "If Miller had bankrupted the game in the Sixties, you could say he didn't improve baseball," he said. "But he didn't, and the game is rolling in dollars today."

Now about Bowie Kuhn. In fairness, he did settle a player boycott when he took over in 1969, opening spring training camps against the owners' wishes to replace major leaguers with scabs. And he did perform a principled, if debatable, act when he vetoed Charlie Finley's attempt to sell off his best players. As the servant of cantankerous owners, Kuhn had limited options. Dealing with the new challenge of united and organized union members baffled ownership and its anointed leader. Stiff and reserved, descended from senators and governors, sometimes referring to himself in the third person, Kuhn stepped out of a time warp. Occasionally he seemed clueless in dealing with contemporary issues. In 1970, he called Jim Bouton into his office to complain about Bouton's book Ball Four, even though many people inside and outside baseball said it was good for the game. In 1971, Kuhn announced the opening of Negro League exhibit in which Satchel Paige would get a plaque; Kuhn adamantly stated that the plaque did not mean Paige had been elected to the Hall. Following cries of "separate but equal!" the commissioner and the Hall director reversed themselves and installed Negro Leaguers in the plaque room with other baseball immortals.

In 1975, baseball arbitrator Peter Seitz all but begged Kuhn to change the reserve clause that bound players to their teams in perpetuity. Seitz couldn't have made his intentions clearer. No doubt Kuhn was swelling over the Supreme Court's 1972 decision

women cover baseball but deprive them of a quote-heavy source? Unthinkable. My friend Melissa Ludtke, then a *Sports Illustrated* reporter, was backed by the magazine as point woman for the case in court. Kuhn lost the 1978 Ludtke v. Kuhn decision, and privacy-conscious players can damn well wear towels.

I never fully understood Kuhn until he had a lunch with *Sports Illustrated* staffers around 1980. A nice man, he encouraged free-ranging conversation. At one point, I made a passionate plea for action on eliminating beanballs. I even might have suggested that when intent is clear, pitchers should be arrested and charged for assault with a deadly weapon!

If you think I sound unhinged, consider what Adam Felder wrote in theatlantic.com: "Throwing a baseball at 90 miles per hour or more at another human being qualifies as 'assault with a deadly weapon.' It's only between the foul lines that a violent felony is instead viewed as enforcing the game's unwritten rules."

"We'll take care of that, Jim," the commissioner said. I'm still waiting.

I also went on about how nighttime postseason games were depriving youngsters and oldsters of the chance to see contests to the end. "I'm not sure that's the case," Kuhn said.

The wording in Kuhn's Hall of Fame plaque reads:

"Baseball's fifth commissioner presided over astounding growth in the game's popularity. With a proactive and inventive administration under his leadership, tripled major league attendance. Extended postseason with creation of the league championship series and introduced night-time baseball to the World Series. Expanded television coverage with dual network broadcasts and a variety of baseball programming. Known as a tough disciplinarian, also a strong supporter of amateur baseball. Instrumental in the Hall of Fame's 1971 decision to induct Negro League players."

"One of my duties as a Hall of Fame library researcher was to copy-edit and critique proposed plaque text for newly elected Hall of Famers," Gabriel Schechter, now a baseball writer, blogger and researcher, wrote on his blog. "I pointed out several inaccuracies in the proposed text for Kuhn, who was apparently being immortalized for things he didn't do. I am chagrined to report that my suggested changes were not adopted, and the inaccuracies remain on the plaque that is hanging in the main gallery of the Hall of Fame museum in Cooperstown.

"When the person who wrote the original text described Kuhn's administration as 'proactive and inventive,' I wrote a note in the margin asking for some clarification of what those adjectives meant when applied to Kuhn, and requested some specific examples of what was meant. I'm still waiting for a response apart from the fact that those vague adjectives made it onto the final plaque. If you read a book like John Helyar's *Lords of the Realm*, you get a portrait of Kuhn as a man who fought progress and innovation on almost every front. He led the battle against the reserve clause and kept his head firmly planted in the sand on nearly every issue involving the balance of power between the owners and players. This was perfectly understandable: he was hired by the owners and owed his power to Walter O'Malley and the other owners who actually ran the game."

Schechter continued: "Let's look at some of the other [proposed] statements on Kuhn's plaque. The one I fought the hardest to delete was the claim that under Kuhn, 'baseball expanded from 20 to 24 teams, league championship series grew postseason...'

The first part of that simply is *not* so, and the second part is garbled. Kuhn's tenure as commissioner began in February, 1969. The expansion from 20 to 24 teams occurred in 1969, as did the institution of divisional play and the second tier of playoffs, the LCS [League Championship Series], which preceded the World Series. The Hall of Fame would like us to believe that Kuhn created all of

"Another statement of purported fact on the plaque is the assertion that Kuhn 'tripled major-league attendance' during his tenure (1969–1984). That simply isn't true. In 1962, the first year when there were 20 major-league teams, MLB attendance totaled 22,519,278. That's a little over 1.1 million per team. Attendance in the 1960s peaked at a little over 25 million in 1966; and in 1968, the last year before Kuhn became commissioner, it was 23,102,745. That was still less than 1.2 million per team.

"The highest attendance during Kuhn's tenure was 45,540,302, in 1983. In his final year, 1984, attendance was 44,742,863. These figures are less than twice the figures from 1968, so how this translates into *tripling* attendance is beyond me. Moreover, by the 1980s the majors had expanded from 20 to 26 teams. The average attendance in 1984 was roughly 1.7 million per team. That's barely a 50% increase over 1968. That's way further from tripling attendance (or 300%, for those of you keeping score at home) than the total figure. But that's what his plaque in Cooperstown says he did. Huh?

"In fact, it was Kuhn's poor business record which caused owners to oust him in 1984. As Expos owner Charles Bronfman put it (quoted in Helyar's book), 'the economics of the industry were in bad shape and Bowie wouldn't do anything to help. As salaries started to escalate, you had to improve revenue streams.'

Gee, it sounds as though MLB needed a commissioner who was 'proactive and inventive' to come in and save the day, because Kuhn was neither of those things. So they hired Peter Ueberroth, who proved to be proactive and inventive by instituting the collusion policy which later cost MLB some $280 million in lawsuits. But that's another story.

"I'm far from the first observer to point out that Bowie Kuhn being in the Hall of Fame while Marvin Miller is not, is the biggest travesty of recent baseball history. It's that simple, and it definitely constitutes fraudulent history. Nobody has had a bigger influence on the past 40 years of baseball than Miller. What Branch Rickey did for African-American ballplayers, Miller did for *all* ballplayers. He freed them. He liberated them over the strident protests of Kuhn and the owners that he would *kill* baseball by doing so. Say what you want about the balance of power possibly tipping too far in the players' favor in recent years. Maybe it's 60–40% in favor of the players today, and that might or might not be a good thing. Before Miller took over, it was 100–0% in favor of the owners, an evil only he was patient and shrewd enough to overcome. For that, he should've been elected 20 years ago."

If you think I've belabored the Kuhn/Miller dichotomy, there's a reason. In a fast-changing society whose social views have liberalized, baseball is embarrassingly conservative and anachronistic. Behaviorally, it's not cool enough to attract enough young fans and especially minority fans. Philosophically, reverence for history is very nice; but modern thinking is better. I said I would be constructive, so here are five changes I think baseball should make:

- No surprise here. Once intent is established—admittedly, that won't be easy—arrest pitchers who throw beanballs or other "purpose pitches" that hit batters. If managers ordered the beanballs, they too should be arrested.

- To avoid beanbrawls, suspend any batter who rushes the mound for 20 games.

- Extend the protective netting all the way to the foul poles, by which I mean anywhere a fan could be struck by a line drive without time to duck. After two near-fatal incidents—a woman hit by a bat fragment, a man struck by a foul ball—the commissioner's office in 2015 recommended protective netting that extends from the backstop 70 feet down each baseline to the near edge of the dugout. Every team has complied or already had the recommended netting, and the Twins, Royals and Nationals have extended the netting to the far side of the dugout. Th

should go to court on privacy grounds.

• Play all World Series games in the afternoon. Thus will youngsters and oldsters see the game in real time. Thus will the Fall Classic resume its blissfully transgressive effect on workplaces and schools. And here's the kicker: Afternoon games won't have significantly lower TV ratings than night games. If you don't believe me, Google "The National Past(bed)time" for a *Sports Illustrated* column on restoring daytime Series games by Jane Bachman Wulf.

Some more radical ideas abound like three balls for a walk and two strikes for a strikeout. Free-flowing debate flourishes, and baseball does make needed changes, however belatedly. Ballpark seats and cuisine are vastly improved. Instant replay challenges reduce the likelihood that umpires' mistakes will be pivotal. (See: Game Six of the 1985 World Series.) The addition of a second wild-card team in each league and a one-game playoff between the two give more incentive to winning the division and avoiding a sudden-death matchup. Catchers are more protected from jarring collisions by Rule 7.13, now that runners can't deviate from their path to make contact with catchers or others covering home plate. Chase Utley's rolling-block slide that famously broke shortstop Ruben Tejada's leg in the 2015 postseason has given way to Rule 6.01(j), which requires runners to execute a "bona fide" slide making contact with the ground before reaching the base; attempting to touch the base with hand or foot, not changing path to make contact with the fielder, and not sliding past the base And umpires have been told to watch the "neighborhood play" more carefully, signaling safe if the fielder doesn't touch the base while turning the pivot on double plays.

The game always seems to rescue itself with magic just when it's needed most. The best thing that could happen to baseball in 2015 was the Kansas City Royals winning the World Series against the New York Mets. Of the 30 major-league teams, the Royals had the 16th highest payroll. The idea that only the richest teams dominate can now exit to an unmarked grave. Other clubs spent endlessly on lights-out starting pitchers and sluggers. The Royals had neither. Benefiting from revenue sharing that improves competitive balance, they scouted well and built patiently from the draft. Then the Royals won with a combination of contact hitters, sharp relief pitching, great fielding, accent on fundamentals (a forgotten art) and heads-up baseball. Hey, this is a team that studied the tendencies of umpires!

Two alert plays gladdened the hearts of baseball lovers everywhere. Let's start with the American League Championship Series against Toronto. With the score tied 2–2 in the eighth inning of Game Six (the Royals leading, three games to two), KC's Lorenzo Cain led off by drawing a walk. When Eric Hosmer singled to right, Cain was on his way to third routinely. Then two things happened. First, right fielder Jose Bautista lollipopped his throw to second. Immediately, third-base coach Mike Jirschele gave Cain the whirling right-arm signal to go home. Cain easily beat the throw.

Note that Cain was running hard to third, even though he was sure to get there unmolested. Note further that Jirschele saw Bautista's throw and made the instant calculation that Cain could score. It was the winning run that sent the Royals to the World Series.

In the ninth inning of the Series' Game Four, the Mets were leading 2–1, with Hosmer on third and one out. Salvador Perez grounded toward the shortstop hole, but third baseman David

Wright cut off the ball. Wright checked Hosmer, who was edging down the line, then threw to first. The moment the ball left Wright's hand, Hosmer made a mad dash toward home. First baseman Lucas Duda caught Wright's throw to get Perez but uncorked a wild throw home, allowing Hosmer to score. "They keep finding ways!" Joe Buck called out on television. Hosmer knew that

O brave new world, / That has such people in it!

ACKNOWLEDGMENTS

Back in the summer of 2015, I received an email from Howie Moffett, chairman of the *Yale Daily News* when I was working there. Would I like to contribute an essay on sports for the 50th-reunion Class Book? It was a perfect opportunity to do something

love to be enlightened about a sport so central to the American experience. Did I have enough for a book? I decided that I had articles from my years at *Sports Illustrated* and beyond that I'd like to republish, and plenty of ideas to write about the current state of the game. I hadn't done much for Yale, but Yale had done something major for me.

Ira Berkow, John S. Bowman, Duke Goldman and Gabriel Schechter gave the manuscript critical reads. Paul Laliberte copy-edited everything except the pieces from *Sports Illustrated* and the *Philadelphia Inquirer Magazine* that I got permission to publish in toto. Too many people contributed to the Ron Taylor "bonus piece" to be named; but special thanks go to Toby Condliffe for introducing me to the great man, and to Ron himself, Ron's wife Rona and their sons Drew and Matthew. Other contributors include Bill Ryczek, Steve Wulf, Buster Olney, Howard Nenner and Andy Zimbalist, as well as my wife Brooks Robards for editing articles over the years that grew into chapters.

I wish to thank Vince Scilla for gracing the cover of *Clearing the Bases* with his haunting painting *Skyfall*.

Last but by no means least, a special thank-you to Zane Kotker for introducing me to Steve Strimer at Levellers Press. If I've forgotten anyone, I owe you a ballpark hot dog.